THEY DON'T CALL IT THE
SUBMISSION
PROCESS

for Nothing

A Rookie Author's Rookie Year

By

Prioleau Alexander

BLYDYN SQUARE BOOKS
KENILWORTH, NJ

DEDICATION

For my bride Heidi,
who's been dealing with
the ups and downs of
my serial typing for
over two decades.

Cover and Interior design by Gram Telen
www.**fiverr**.com/gramtelen

TABLE OF CONTENTS

"Writing is its own reward."

Henry Miller

For Jimmy -
Thank you for the
ride - you are the
only person who'll
ever knows what
this means!

INTRODUCTION

Aspiring authors are haunted by one primary question: *How do I get published?* A close second is: *What would it be like … if I **could** get published?*

Signing a deal with a traditional publishing house is a painful task—mostly because it includes shoving yourself face-first into the soul chipper called "the submission process," and being torn to shreds by ego-crushing rejections. Many brilliant writers remain forever undiscovered, as they collapse under the weight of the process. Believe me, I understand … but such is the nature of things.

I was lucky/blessed enough to become a traditionally published author, but even so, I would answer the first question—*How do I get published?*—by saying: "I have no idea. I don't even know how *I* got published." In reality, I'd bet 90 percent of traditionally published authors would say the same thing.

This is not a joke. Having your manuscript selected for publication is a tangled mess of luck, timing, what's selling, who's buying, and whether the person reading your manuscript or pitch letter is hungover. Odds are excellent that a manuscript reader overcome with heartache because her fiancé just dumped her at the altar won't be much in the mood to read your manuscript entitled *I'm in Love and I'm So Happy*.

Seriously: If you submitted a brilliant, well-written, interesting, compelling, sure-to-be-successful manuscript … and it got rejected, odds are it was just bad luck. If your *I'm in Love* manuscript landed on the desk of a newlywed, things probably would've been different, no?

The examples of rejections in a variety of genres are legion: *Harry Potter* was rejected 12 times; *Gone with the Wind*, 38 times; *Twilight*, 14 times; *Chicken Soup for the Soul*, 144 times; *Dune*, 23 times.

Personally, I'd argue that *Chicken Soup* should've been rejected infinity times, but who am I to judge?

Those are some seriously talented folks listed there (except the *Chicken Soup* dude). Know what happened to finally get them published? Their blood-sweat-tears manuscript landed on the right desk, at the right time, in front of the right person, at a moment in time when that genre was selling.

This reality check probably won't make your own rejections feel any less painful—writers are, by and large, sensitive souls. But know this: Rejections can often *feel* personal, even though they are not.

Okay, enough of that. Let's move on to the second question: *What would it be like if I could get published?* This is a question that a published author actually can answer, but most beg off. After all, leaking that information would free unpublished writers from the pain of obsessing over the mystery of published writers' personal success and what their lives are like.

Authors like the idea of being Oz behind the curtain. If you are an aspiring author, you likely believe the lives of published writers are filled with stimulating intellectual discussions with other authors, sipping red wine on the West Bank, a bottomless checkbook, and legions of fans fighting with broken bottles to buy them a drink.

To avoid destroying that fantasy, published writers will almost always answer the what-is-it-like question—delivering the reply over the top of reading glasses—with something like, "It's rewarding. Yes, rewarding."

If an eager fan pushes for a deeper answer, the author might give a slight chuckle and say, "Well, it's not all it appears to be."

Let me tell you: Truer words have never been spoken.

Before We Get Started ...

So, you want to know what it's like to get traditionally published? I can certainly offer you some answers to Frequently Asked Questions:

1. **Is it fun?** At times, yes. I mean, it's not skydiving fun, but on good days it can be ... actually, let's hold off on this one. I've got a bit of a tale to share, so you can be the one who decides on the definition of *fun*.

2. **Is it exciting?** Sure. I mean, it's not *riding on a roller-coaster assembled yesterday in the rain by a seventeen-year-old carnie who'd just finished his fourth bong hit of Pineapple Express* level exciting, but it's pretty cool seeing your book in a bookstore.

3. **Is it rewarding?** To some degree. Remember those times in college when you did those eye exercises to increase your reptilian vision, then sat next to the smart dude in the third row and came out of the finals with an A-plus? That's rewarding, right? Of course it was. It's like that.

4. **Will I get rich?** If you base it on rookie author statistics, the answer is no. Hell, no. But you could meet a dreamy guy/gal at a bar where you're smashing martinis trying to summon the strength to endure yet another book signing and end up rich in love.

5. **How will I know when I've found "my voice"?** When you've practiced writing so much you're on your third computer, you're getting there.

6. **Why do you write?** Because I can't *not* write. If you find writing to be less than an obsession, stop. Trust me: There be dragons here.

7. **Will it fill the hole in my heart/provide me with a feeling of validation/make me the center of attention at every party/make everything in my life perfect?** No, a little, no, and lol.

If you're reading these ramblings, odds are you're serious about your craft and are damn sure determined to get your manuscript published. I applaud you, as actually finishing a manuscript is a very rare accomplishment.

You should know, however, that I'm not writing to tell you *how* to get published. Again, I have no idea. It's sort of like walking out of an airliner crash and you emerge as the only survivor, still carrying your cookie and one-third-cup of apple juice. What happened? Why you? Who the hell knows?

I suppose if there's one piece of advice I could offer—and take it with a grain of salt—it's to consider what genre you work in. Is it crime fiction? Okay, that's cool. How is your crime fiction different from what's on the market? There are probably a hundred very successful crime-fiction writers on the market, and they're typing as fast as they can to get their next book into the rodeo.

How is your crime-fiction novel going to bully its way into the public's collective view?

Well, perhaps there's the style of your voice. If you want to read crime fiction by an author with a cult following, read Andrew Vachss. His characters are sometimes cartoonish, but his style of writing is stunning and his topics are raw and painful to touch. Mostly, his books are about the protagonist, Burke, hunting down and murdering pedophiles. That's a plot no one can disagree with.

There's the combo of plot and characters. To find some insanely fun examples of this, read Carl Hiaasen and Tim Dorsey. For sheer creativity, read Christopher Moore—he's not a crime-fiction writer, but he knows how to bring a character to life like no one else.

I think we can all agree that John Grisham owns the lawyer-is-a-good-guy thriller sector. My opinion is his stuff should be filed under fantasy, but millions of people love it. Can you pirate some of his readers who can suspend their belief enough to view lawyers as good-guy-heroes? Hmm ... perhaps. But perhaps you could make your lawyer a drug-addicted, mob-connected, thrice-divorced narcissist who dances in a drag show every other Saturday. I'd read that book.

Another example of a unique approach would be Everett De Morier, who wrote his novel *Thirty-three Cecils* relying heavily on great dialogue—and as a twist, he wrote the fictional tale as if it centered on a real-life news story.

My point is this: If your crime-fiction book is about a murder and the detectives solving it, why use a gun for the murder? Why not a javelin, with the coup de grâce delivered by a shotput? You don't need to rewrite your book to make a change: Same everything, but the primary suspect is a high-school track coach and the killer is the second runner-up for homecoming queen who blames him for her loss of the crown. Play it serious, or play it funny—I'd read that book.

Why shouldn't one of your cops be a seven-foot former basketball star with Tourette's syndrome and a black belt in Brazilian judo? Why couldn't your killer be a perpetually horny vampire, whom the cops shoot time and again, but keeps getting away? Why not have a love interest who is a past-her-prime movie star who keeps getting recognized and screws up the detective's attempts to remain in the shadows?

Oh, and hear me when I offer this chunk of advice: Your first page better be the best first page of any book ever written. Writers like you and I don't enjoy the luxury of "having a few chapters" for the story to build. You must sell the book based on the first page ... then resell it based on the second page ... then continue that process for every page until reaching the part that reads, "The End."

My goal here is to help you to understand what occurs after you get published—what goes on behind that magical and mysterious curtain, separating you from the seemingly untouchable "published authors." From there, you can decide if the juice is worth the squeeze.

If you want to learn more about how to get published, I recommend *Secrets Most Writers and Publishers Will Never Tell You* by Tara Tomczyk. She will provide you with both a reality check and some pointers and ideas you'll find nowhere else.

If you're still with me, put on your helmet, tie off your flashlight, double-check your ropes, and don't forget your water: We're going spelunking deep into the heart of the publishing experience. I can't tell you what you'll see or hear down there, but I can point out what areas of the cave I've seen. What you carry out of this cave will be up to you.

THE SILENT ART

Art, in general, is a confusing and overused term. After all, what is art? We all agree Michelangelo's works are art, but does merely holding a paintbrush in your hand make you an artist? Does playing "second bunny" in your kindergarten play make you an actor? Heady stuff.

The process by which an artist transforms from "writer" to "published author" is probably the least understood of all artistic endeavors, and without a doubt, the most difficult of all.

It's much easier to understand the process of going from "musician" to "recording artist," because if you're a good musician, and you get yourself some gigs, and the crowds increase in size, and people talk about you, and girls you don't know are suddenly hanging around, then there's at least *a chance* that a music label will wander into a show and consider your potential. Musicians are also fortunate because, in order to enjoy the fun of being a "musician," they never actually need to transition from "musician" to "recording artist." They can simply stand on a street corner, play some tunes, and let people walking by listen, whether they like it or not. Credit for this goes to the Doppler effect.

Same goes for an actor. You can act in local theater or spend a couple of hours at happy hour, then bellow Hamlet's monologue on a street corner until the cops come; all the world's your stage, no?

We writers, however, live in a different world. A writer seeking publication is an "imagination egotist" who sits alone at a computer, pecking out the details of some sort of story, hoping others will want to read it. Writing the first draft requires an investment of hundreds of hours, and that's only after the thousands of hours you practiced developing your voice. When the draft is done and you've honed it to a razor sharpness ... well, what now? Let me tell you, amigo—few things are uglier than a big, thick, unpublished manuscript. Why? Because of the time investment required to read it.

Let's consider a musician saddled with this same dilemma. He's been writing an album of songs over the past eight months, and now he's ready to play for an actual listener. Imagine if he was faced with the same amount of time it takes to read a manuscript:

GUITARIST: Hey, Mom! I've been practicing for the past eight months. Want to hear my stuff?

MOM: Sure, hon ...

GUITARIST: Okay, but there's one small caveat.

MOM: What's that?

GUITARIST: I'm coming over every night for two weeks, and each night I'll play for three hours, but you can't comment until I've completed the entire set.

MOM: Son ... that would be great. But I've got to go to the doctor.

GUITARIST: What doctor?

MOM: Kevorkian.

Or how about a painter caught in the writer's world:

PAINTER: Hey, Mike! My old college roomie! Sup?

MIKE: I'm good. What's up, dude?

PAINTER: Man, I'm having my first art showing! You in?

MIKE: Cool! Where's it gonna be?

PAINTER: At your house. I'm going to come by every night for two weeks, and each night you'll sit in silence while I spend two hours discussing the paintings: the technique, the inspiration, how they make me feel, how they should make you feel—you know, the usual.

MIKE: Dude, I wish I could, but I've committed to attending a multilevel marketing meeting. They're selling time shares in Kosovo, and I'm giddy about going bankrupt.

No matter how you slice it, the journey to become an author or accomplished writer is a long, strange, exhausting hike. If you tell someone you've spent the past *two years* writing a manuscript, it's amazing how often you'll hear a reply along the lines of, "Really? I've got a great idea for a book myself, if I could just find time to write it."

If you say to the same person that you've spent the past two years perfecting Handel's *Messiah*, the odds are extremely low that they will respond, "You know, I've been meaning to perfect Beethoven's Sixth myself, but I haven't been able to find the time to learn the piano."

No, they will likely look impressed and ask, "Will you play it for me?"

So, what is a writer to do? There is only one answer: Get published. And how hard can that be, right?

Good question.

How Hard It Can Be ...

At the time I was struggling to win over an agent—this was twenty years ago, when dinosaurs still roamed the Earth—one single icon emerged as the symbol of the quest. Unlike the Holy Grail, this particular symbol was easy to find, and unlike Ahab's great white whale, there was no peril in attaining it. In fact, it's available right down the road at your neighborhood post office. This hallowed jewel was known as the *self-addressed, stamped envelope.*

The self-addressed, stamped envelope was such a unique and ubiquitous part of the journey to publication that it morphed into an acronym among those in the biz, and we called it, simply, the SASE. Every single literary agent who was open to interacting with new talent listed the SASE as the most important element within a submission package.

"I wonder why?" I remember thinking while perusing my library of "How to Get Published" books. "Maybe it's so they can quickly and easily send me my advance."

No, no. That's not quite it. Literary agents are *not* seeking a more efficient way to begin their professional relationship with you. The truth is a bit more nuanced. You see, the sad reality is that *SASE* doesn't stand for "self-addressed, stamped envelope." It actually stands for "Sorry, Ass-monkey. Send Elsewhere."

Yes, I'm afraid it's true. Due to the sheer volume of rejection letters that agents sent out every day, they required the submitter to pay for their own dream-crushing freight. By way of an analogy, imagine a loan shark calling to say he'll be by next Tuesday to kick your ass, but he needs an advance to pay for the dry-cleaning of his soon-to-be-bloody suit. For a struggling writer, that's what the SASE became.

Rejection letters came back in many forms. Or, in my experience, many, *many* forms. The nicer ones—which felt like, oh, just a ninja throwing-star to the Adam's apple—came on the agent's official letterhead and used phrases like, "We are unable to give your work the attention it so richly deserves." The not-so-nice rejections ... well, they stung a little more. Imagine submitting your Great American Novel to an agent, and three months later, you receive one-third of a sheet of paper, hand-cut and crooked, a copy of a copy of a copy, that starts off: "Due to the volume of queries we receive ... " For me, that qualified as a baseball-cleats vasectomy, without a bag of frozen peas for the post-op.

Yes, today the biz uses email, but there was just something about those envelopes that made rejection even more painful. Maybe because it involved more effort? I don't know. But I don't miss those days.

Of course, in those days, agents and publishers had to actually stuff the SASE and mail it, so that indicates some sort of relationship, right? I mean, they actually took time personally to shatter your dreams, so that's something. Today, it's much easier and less personal. They just: a) hit auto-reply, b) delete your document, and c) block your email address.

Anyway, one thing hasn't changed: the rejections. Why are we writers rejected on such a frequent basis by these agents?

Have sympathy: *Agents have the worst job on the planet.*

Imagine, if you will, committing several hours a day to reading poorly written, disjointed, mind-numbing fiction. Then let's season that salad with a few volumes of bad poetry. Add the occasional biography of someone's grandpa who fought in World War II and went on to become a philosopher-janitor. Finally, let's top it all off with a manuscript from every single yo-yo this poor literary agent has ever met at a cocktail party, no matter how briefly.

People, this isn't a job; it's hell, in a Word document.

Would You Want to Be An Agent? Or a Publisher?

Here's the painful, statistical truth: As writers, you and I probably suck. Except no one ever tells us we suck. If you write a romance novel about Renaissance England and show it to your husband, what do you think he's going to say? That it's boring? This man wants to have sex with you at some point in the next decade. Or how about the guy who writes a thriller about robbing a spa/salon? Do you think wifey-poo is *really* going to tell him the truth? With that new ottoman hanging in the balance? Not a chance.

So, the literary agents and publishers are stuck being the ones who have to tell us we suck.

And this is where the disconnect occurs. None of us want *our* writing to be part of those statistics ... the mass of aspiring writers whose work is rejected. We pour our hearts into the keyboard, and whether the book ends up being good or bad, it still takes hundreds of hours of soul-sucking effort and passion. As an added torture nugget, if you're like me, you can't imagine "maturing" or getting better as a writer simply by writing more.

Come on! My first manuscript was awesome! It's ready for prime time! No matter how many years of practice I put in, I'll never top that brilliance! I ... do ... not ... suck.

Every other writer might suck, but *we* don't, right? I, for one, can describe a "heaving breast" like no one ever before or since. My bad guys aren't just bad; they are *symbolic Iago-ish icons* of the good-and-evil duality of humanity, the likes of which hasn't been explored so brilliantly since *Blood Meridian*. And if the damn reader would just stick with the manuscript through the first hundred and seventy pages and allow the story to build, they'd see I'm quite possibly the next James Joyce.

News flash: Here is how much money the agent who discovers the next James Joyce will make: zero. Here is how much the agent will make who convinces Oprah to put her name on a cookbook she's never even laid eyes on: one gazillion dollars.

You see, for agents to make money, they have to sell the book to a publishing house. For a publishing house to make money, they must then print and sell those books to readers. Now, which do you think will sell more copies? The cookbook with Oprah's photo on it, where she swears she stays thin with no effort? Or your "important" novel that explores the relationship between adopted twins and cuts deep down into the issues of self, selfishness, and selflessness? Hint: Are there more people looking for a no-effort solution for thinness, or adopted twins seeking someone to understand them?

If you're still confused, ask yourself this question: If Americans won't even commit two hours to an "important" movie, will an "important" four-hundred-page book fare any better? That doesn't mean "don't write your important novel," but it does mean "consider what you're up against."

Goal number one for those in the publishing business is to get successful authors to type as fast as possible—because people buy their books. Even if they write a stinker, people will still buy it. Please point out a famous author who hasn't written at least one book that, when you finish reading it, you wondered if they were drunk when they wrote it. When a really successful author emerges, publishers will maximize profits to the point that they convince these writers to even switch to an easier genre like kids' books or cookbooks, just to get crap with their name on it out onto the street faster. Hell, if it would result in enough quick cash, the writer and publisher would probably agree to slapping their name on a book of crossword puzzles.

Right behind proven-successful authors in the pecking order of "getting published" come online digital celebrities. If you have a podcast, YouTube, or TikTok channel with a million followers, publishers smell blood in the water. If even one percent of your followers buy a copy of your book—which you will hawk endlessly on your platform—

that's ten thousand books. That's enough for the publisher to make a little dough. You, of course, will make next to jack-nothing, but that's another story.

Then, there are the TV/movie/reality-show celebrity "writers." Forgive me, but I don't have the energy right now to describe that cesspool of humanity and the trees they kill.

And finally ... there's you and me. Way down in the taking-a-big-risk category when the publisher is evaluating options for new books to publish.

Believe me when I say that I understand your frustration at the industry's unwillingness to take a chance on us unknown writers. Somehow, it seems like that should be their goal: to discover new talent. But for the big publishing houses, it ain't. These are companies with thousands of employees, and NYC rent, and overhead, and hard costs, and travel budgets—it's seriously big business.

There *are* smaller publishing houses who are in it "for the love of the art," but you've got to do some serious detective work to find the ones that are interested in your genre. A lot of them are actually looking for you ... *if* you've found your writing voice ... *if* you understand what a big deal you aren't ... *if* your topic is appealing to a large enough audience ... *if* your submission forces them to drink coffee all night because they don't want to stop reading ... *if* you understand that your submission is so far from flawless that it might as well be written on a tablet with a Big Chief crayon.

If you do find a small publishing house that seems to be a good fit for you, hold your damn horses. These people are busy. Get down on your knees and beg friends and family to be critical of your manuscript. If they won't do it, join a writing group and beg someone to be a "beta reader." If you can't manage that, bribe a high school English teacher.

Why? Because you want the first draft that small publisher sees to be the best work you've ever produced. You need it to be so good, they feel inspired to take a risk. Measure yourself against the best books you've ever read in your genre … then you're ready.

Above all else, keep this in mind: No matter how brilliant your writing is, fearless persistence is your job when you're a writer seeking a small-press publisher or a literary agent. One rejection isn't a no. Twenty rejections isn't a no. A hundred rejections—okay, a hundred rejections is saying something. Either your first chapter sucks, or your writing sucks, or your topic sucks, or … hell, I don't know. Something sucks.

My Strike One

My first manuscript explored the trials of turning thirty. Part-truth and part-fiction, it offered a humorous account of two friends and me traveling through Europe, struggling with the concept of reaching the big three-zero, and having to become real, no-kidding-around adults. (At the time, thirty seemed old.) When I reached the end of this exhaustive typing exercise, I gave the manuscript to a dozen friends and family, and got solid reviews. The broad consensus was that it was, at the very least, laugh-out-loud funny. In my opinion, the manuscript defied the statistical suckage and deserved publication.

Next stop: my acquisition of several "How to Get Published" books. As mentioned earlier, this is where the self-addressed, stamped envelope came into play, but that was only the beginning. "How to Get Published" books provide a very specific formula for attracting a very busy agent's attention, and inform you that straying from this formula will doom you faster than winning the lotto and discovering a taste for uncut Bolivian marching powder in the same weekend. Here's a short version of the formula:

Dear (Agent's Name):

With great self-loathing and humility, I beseech that thee taketh a look at my musings. Yea, though my scribblings be not worthy for thine eyes to behold, I feel it my bounden duty to present them to thee. I believe you'll like it because

_____.

With great thanksgiving,
(Your Name)

The blank space is where you would describe how your book is unique and destined to sell more copies than, say, that cookbook Oprah agreed to smile for. Perhaps you wrote it without using verbs. Or maybe you shattered the current record for heaving-breasts-per-page. Maybe you drew Vonnegut-style cartoons of Muhammad and are ready to go into bestseller exile. Whatever the angle, it better be good. In my case, the angle was that my manuscript was a right-of-passage book that wasn't all angst-filled and boo-hoo-hoo. I thought it filled a pretty interesting, underserved niche, in a non-sucky way.

Only a wormhole in the space-time continuum could account for how quickly the SASE rejections piled into my mailbox. In fact, one was already waiting for me when I returned from dropping off the initial mailing at the post office. And they *kept* coming. I didn't keep an exact count, but I'm fairly confident three rejections materialized for every query letter I sent out.

Once again, I scrutinized the "How to Get Published" books, and their advice was clear: *Don't give up! Press on! You don't suck, even if you suck!*

So I did. I pressed on. Then, after playing SASE boomerang for months, it occurred to me that the U.S. Postal Service might be behind these "How to Get Published" books. What could be an easier way to increase their profits? My local mail carrier spies a letter to a literary agency and sets it aside. One day later, he opens it, stuffs the SASE with a rejection note, and drops it by my house. A stamp was purchased, but the letter never left the neighborhood. Genius! Evil, but genius! My wife listened to my theory as I spewed it forth in angry detail. After days of my ranting, she worked the words *trial separation* into the discussion, and the conversation faded toward something like painting the crown molding or getting the dog fixed. But still, I wondered.

My next move involved playing a few of my aces in the hole. Through family connections, some people in the publishing biz kinda-sorta knew my name, so it was time to call in a few favors. Even if these folks couldn't actually pull the trigger on a book deal, they might be able to assuage my ego by telling me what a not-sucky writer I was, and perhaps kick my book upstairs to the decision-makers who had the power to consider it.

Their responses ripped into me like a bear at an all-you-can-maul hunter buffet. One told me, "You need to be more deliberate," as if my chosen style of writing were … what, an accident? Another said, "You need to practice writing more," unaware that my professional job (for ten years) had been as an advertising writer—and that I'd won a couple of dozen awards for the craft they were telling me I now needed to practice. The third opinion was that the book was too "stereotypical Southern male," and thus, "wouldn't sell well." Apparently, us Southern boys is just a bunch of mule humpers, and our kind don't buy nothing that's gots to do with fancy book learnin'.

But let's be real. Why did all those bastards and bastardettes say these mean things that hurt my feelings? Really?

Because my book sucked.

I didn't think so. It was my baby, so of course, I loved it. But now, twenty-five years later, when I go back and read it, with more than two decades of practice? I'm fortunate they didn't drive to my house and give me a knuckle sandwich for wasting their time.

Bruised but not broken, I returned to my stack of "How to Get Published" books, which assured me in no uncertain terms: "Perhaps the topic you chose sucks, and maybe the way you arranged the words sucked, but there's no way *you* suck. Consider purchasing our companion book, *How to Write Better So You Can Become a Published Writer*." The concept struck me as a bit like selling a book to biology majors entitled *How to Be Smarter So You Can Get into Med School*. I subsequently recategorized these books in my mind from "good value" to "suspect."

Having already spent our family emergency fund on SASEs, an idea rose like a Tomahawk missile to my brain: To hell with the old book—just invest a couple of thousand after-work hours writing a book on a new topic! The "How to Get Published" books said that if your book is *good enough*, it's impossible for it *not* to get published. My thinking here demonstrates my affliction with the writer's disease, because if I *really* felt my literary mission involved exploring the angst of turning thirty, then that idea would remain front and center until I achieved perfection, right? Nah. Perfection wasn't the point. The point was publication, publication, publication. And if that meant writing a new book, then one new book was comin' up!

Up to Bat

Okay, the space above, between this paragraph and the previous one, represents the two years I lost writing my next book. A humorous history of the United States, it uncovered lessons we should've learned, but failed to. No fewer than a dozen people told me the manuscript was the funniest thing they'd ever read, declaring, "This is how they should teach history! Kids might actually stay awake!"

The indent before this sentence represents the several months I lost playing SASE boomerang with my second manuscript. I found myself haunted by the idea that I might be in need of more up-to-date versions of the "How to Get Published" books. And then it happened: A real, live, fast-talking, New York literary agent called.

AGENT: Did you write this?

ME: Uh, yeah?

AGENT: This is the funniest stuff I've read in two years, and
I'm gonna sell it, so don't lie to me. Is this your stuff?

ME: Yes.

AGENT: Okay. Send me the rest.

This interaction wasn't what I expected. Doesn't discovery lead to ... compliments? I mean, what if I were fragile? What if I were some sensitive artist, just one mood swing away from cutting my ear off? Or a quirky, reclusive, alcoholic genius who might burn my manuscript rather than endure such a blasé reaction? Confused, I pressed the topic:

ME: So you really liked the book?

AGENT: It's not a book. It's a manuscript. You're not gonna be one of those whiny, needy types, are you?

ME: Nah, that ain't me. I dig your style, dude.

AGENT: Terrific. Why aren't you on the way to the post office?

So, step one was officially complete. The impossible had morphed into the possible. A literary agent now represented me on the mean streets of the Big Apple. He was a player in the game! And he loved my stuff! New York address, big name clients ... I was on my way to the top!

Why They Call It the "Submission" Process

After an infinite amount of time passed, my agent called:

AGENT: All right, ya big sissy, we're going to start submitting your manuscript. And they don't call it the submission process for nothing. I hope you got thick skin, because these people will say what they think.

ME: If there's one thing I know, it's how to be rejected.

AGENT: Funny. All I'm saying is, you don't have dick until you have a deal. And right now, you ain't got dick.

ME: Does that mean I shouldn't have leased the Porsche?

The next eight months rolled out as the slowest, most agonizing months of my life. My agent sent the manuscript out to one publishing company at a time, along with a cover letter endorsement in which he stated, "Maybe I'm weird, but this is the funniest stuff I've read in years." And one by one, the rejections made their way back. Ever sensitive to my feelings, my agent emailed them to me without a word of comment to ease the blow. Now, a rejection, I could handle, but the wording in some of the letters seemed too much to take. In fact, most of them agreed with my agent, and stated, "I've got to agree. This is some of the funniest stuff I've read in a very long time."

Yes! Yes! Go on!

"Unfortunately, this genre isn't selling very well these days, so we're going to have to pass."

Wait! Wait! You're doing it wrong!

You say, "It sucks," and *then* you pass. You don't say, "It's good," and then pass. You're MegaWorld Books! Whatever *you say sells* is what sells! If there's a *problem* with a genre, you *make* the market! I mean, Hollywood starlets are getting published! If *they're* getting shelf space, how can you turn down a book you think is actually good? Are you there, God? It's me, Prioleau.

And Then … Came the Call

AGENT: Well, we gave it our best shot. No takers.

ME: But, but, but, but …

AGENT: Win some, lose some. Hey, I thought your manuscript was good.

ME: But, but, but, but, but …

AGENT: We had a few laughs, though, huh? Good times.

ME: But, but, but, but …

AGENT: Listen, send me something I can sell, okay?

ME: But, but, but, but …

AGENT: Don't be a stranger.

Aaaaaand … click. Dial tone.

That, my friend, is the kind of thing that rocks you on your heels. You find an agent to represent something you wrote, you make the edits and changes they suggest, you get the manuscript looking spiffy and stuff, you go out to the market, and … boom! A swift kick to the place on your body you find most painful to be kicked.

In my case, it was my ego.

I mean, can you imagine?

It's like Ahab standing on the great whale's back and realizing that he left his harpoon in his cabin. Or Jay Gatsby going colorblind, no longer able to see Daisy's dock. Or Forrest Gump having his leg braces stolen. Or Tom Sawyer stumbling in on Becky and Huck mid- … well, you know.

I lived in a daze for quite some time, unable to write, unable to even visit a bookstore. The whole thing devastated me. It reminded me of Tom Sawyer painting the fence and dreading Monday so badly, he almost wished weekends didn't exist, simply to eliminate the coming of Monday.

That bad, I confess.

I'm being vulnerable, see? My publisher told me to be sure this book included my vulnerability, and listening to your publisher is a very, very, very wise thing to do.

STICKS AND STONES MAY BREAK MY BONES

My pit of despair was so deep and dark, the next couple of years revolved mainly around creative denial. Yes, that's an overreaction, but I'd been close! So close! Close enough to wonder what my book cover would look like! Close enough to mention the word *author* when conversing at a cocktail party! Close enough to ... Shut up, Prioleau. Your manuscript got a fair look, and that's the very most you can ask. I was lucky to have that. But still ...

During this time of feeling sorry for myself, I focused on my advertising job, pretended that my work mattered, and watched in silent hell as the owner of a local Goliath Muffler Shop edited the dialogue in my radio spots. *(You know, Prioleau, you don't have the words* Goliath Muffler Shop *in here enough. They told me at the seminar it should be said at least five times.)* Of course, that's just the tiniest example, as my entire day revolved around clients strangling the life out of any idea I laid at their temple of approval.

ME: And at this point, we cut to a guy on stilts, who says—

CLIENT: Stilts? What do stilts have to do with selling cars?

ME: That's the point. We're getting the viewers to—

CLIENT: Stilts have a negative connotation.

ME: A what?

CLIENT: Everyone fell off stilts as a kid. That's a negative.

ME: A negative?

CLIENT: I don't see any price in this script.

ME: Well, if you'll let me—

CLIENT: Where do I walk in? I'm the brand.

ME: You're the what?

CLIENT: The brand. People buy here because they know they can trust Crazy Mike to be the low-price leader, with service after the sale. That's what we've got to sell. You see? That's creative. The "low-price leader with service after the sale." Do you have someone at your agency who trademarks stuff like that? You know, with a little circle C or one of those TMs?

ME: Brilliant idea. I'm on it, Mike.

My literary pursuits during this time dropped to minimal, thus allowing time for the bile associated with my previous two failures to settle. I'd come so damn close with the history book. How could an agent like it, but publishers didn't? To soothe the savage beast in my belly, I'd swing by the bookstore, look for something that looked as good as my brilliant musings, and then smugly leave empty-handed. Sure, I never opened one of those books, but deep inside I knew mine was better. One day, however, the self-help section obstructed my path, and an epiphany struck me: a self-help book! No, better: a *parody* of a self-help book! Genius! Half a dozen of the stupidest-looking titles leapt into my basket, and followed me home.

My Strike Three

My parody of a self-help book wrote itself, not because I don't feel for people struggling with issues, but because I avoided writing about those topics. In the vein of P. J. O'Rourke's book *Modern Manners*, my coaching and wellness program swerved into the insanity lane, out onto the shoulder, and into the lava-filled ravine.

Was it good? You be the judge. Here's a little excerpt of my brilliance regarding relationships.

* * *

As we all know, couples who attempt to mate for life face serious obstacles. They get bored; they change; they get old and wrinkly and disgusting, and people puke at the thought of them doing it.

For some reason, however, millions of couples try again and again. Success comes in the form of shuffleboard, early-bird buffets, and—with luck—keeling over dead before Alzheimer's kicks in.

For these reasons, my happiness and success program cannot address the complex facets of lifetime relationships. There's too much work involved in making two people happy, and my program is based on your achieving happiness. As a result, my advice is based on your current relationship. Remember: It's never too late to divorce and trade in on a trophy!

Finding the Right Mate

The parameters for finding the right mate are different for men and women, because every good relationship involves a giver and a taker. Of course, I want you to be the taker.

Men Seeking Women	**Women Seeking Men**
Men should search for a woman who fits the acronym DANNY:	Women should search for a man who fits the acronym RACHEL:
D — daddy owns a liquor store	R — rich
A — aerobics instructor	A — amply endowed
N — nymphomaniac	C — cuddles after sex
N — never tires of getting you a beer	H — handsome
Y — younger than you	E — EKG report's bad
	L — loves you, even though you keep having sex with your ex

The problem with Danny and Rachel, however, is not hard to figure out. Danny and Rachel want each other, not you and me.

Criticizing Your Partner

Your best bet for happiness in a relationship is to change your partner. Don't accept their quirks and flaws as "special" or "unique," because that's a defeatist attitude. They *can* change if they *love* you, but you've got to be willing to help them ... again, and again, and again!

Did your dog sit the first time you said, "Sit?" "Roll over?" "Get the paper?"

Then what makes you think your partner will make the bed the first time you ask? Or put down the toilet seat? Or leave you alone when your favorite television show is on?

The key to change is an ongoing program of criticism. Often, the criticism will be issue-specific; other times it will be general criticism to simply mold their self-confidence into a more manageable package. Either way, there are some basic parameters for maximizing your efforts:

Hit them when they least expect it. The most appropriate time is when they are in a good mood:

Example:

WOMAN: Wow, I had a great time tonight!

MAN: Me, too. If only that dress didn't make you look so chunky.

Example:

MAN: I knocked 'em dead in that meeting!

WOMAN: Great! Does that mean your salary might get raised to enough for us to live on?

Be vague and general. It gets them thinking across a broader spectrum.

Example:

WOMAN: Are you happy in our relationship?

MAN: Happy? Of course I'm happy in our relationship. Otherwise, I'd be out in bars pretending to care what some woman has to say.

Example:

MAN: Will you still love me when this bald spot gets bigger?

WOMAN: Well, that's a couple of years from now. Who knows if we'll even still be together?

Bring up generalities that can have only one meaning ... but hide behind the fact you didn't say them.

- "Do you wish you'd taken cooking classes?"
- "Wouldn't it have been great if, when you were sixteen, an older woman had taught you how to make love to a woman?"
- "Wouldn't it be fun to have furniture that's not all worn out?
- "I wonder if it hurts to get breast implants."

- "You know, I read today that lots of men are getting liposuction."

Dig up examples from the past.

"Oh? You never do that? What about the time four years ago on our way to Baltimore when we stopped at that gas station?"

Be sure to reduce things to their most emotional level. Superficial criticism never gets you anywhere. Go overboard every time.

". . . and I'm telling you this because your behavior hurts me bad—cuts me deep! Makes me feel worthless and weak! Where are those sleeping pills?"

Remember the 3 Rs: Repetition Reaps Results.

- Did you take out the garbage?
- Did you take out the garbage?
- Did you take out the garbage?
- Did you take out the garbage?

Never reward a desired behavior ... expect it!

"You took out the garbage? It's about time."

Refuse to clarify. It gives them a way to respond.

"What do I mean, exactly? You know what I mean, exactly. I believe I was speaking English."

Allude to your past. Let's say you and your mate have just finished a two-hour sex session that included standing up in a hammock, trapeze rigging, and a leather face mask with a zipper mouth. You don't want your mate feeling too confident about themselves, so you say:

"You know, one of these days we'll need to do something wild."

And finally, don't let your partner criticize you without some form of counterattack. No matter how small the criticism, you must respond. Otherwise, they may develop a habit that may prove irritating.

Examples:

WOMAN: Honey, your bowtie is crooked.

MAN: Yeah? Well, your new haircut looks stupid.

MAN: Honey, I think my potato is undercooked.

WOMAN: Yeah? Well, my last boyfriend was better than you in bed.

* * *

Again, I thought it was brilliant—and all these years later during a reread, it still makes me laugh. Seriously.

When you're a humorist, your stuff makes you laugh for a while, but eventually you've read it enough. My self-help book still makes me laugh.

Everyone I know who reads it laughs. So I sent it to my agent. After a couple weeks of silence, I made the dreaded call.

ME: Hey, man! What'd you think?

AGENT: About what?

ME: My self-help book, dude!

AGENT: Oh, yeah. I read it. On the can. Why did you write it?

ME: It's funny! It's original!

AGENT: So you think I can sell it?

ME: Yeah.

AGENT: Huh. Maybe that's why I have my job and you don't. If you'd taken five minutes to do some research, you'd have found there aren't any self-help parody books on the market. Wonder why? Do you think you're the first person to ever have the idea? You ain't. There aren't any parody self-help books because ... anyone? Anyone? Bueller? Because they don't sell.

ME: So what you're telling me here is ... make sure there's an interest in a specific genre before writing a book? Is that what you're subtly hinting at?

AGENT: You learn fast there, Marine.

ME: Alexander … out.

Out, Indeed

Why on Earth does anyone want to be a writer? I just couldn't get right with my dream. A musician, sure—sex, drugs, and rock'n'roll. A painter, sure—people look over your shoulder as you work and comment on your talent. An actor, why not—you pretend to be someone else for a couple of hours and people clap. A writer? Hell, it takes me two hours to get my software to indent correctly … and trust me, there aren't any groupies twerking in admiration of proper formatting. In fact, there's a standing joke in Hollywood that goes, "That's a starlet so stupid, she slept with the writer."

The lunacy of my dream washed over me like the darkness over The Dude. And in that darkness, on the edge of that abyss, I came to grips with what a time-wasting pursuit writing was—and convinced myself it wasn't a dream worth chasing. I became Springsteen, down by the river. John Galt, working the subway rails. Charlie Croker, reading the works of the Stoics. Skip Wiley, surrendering his beloved Everglades to the developers.

It was, indeed, Alexander … out.

Hey, Hold My Beer. I Wanna Try Something …

The curse of the creative mind is this: There's only a very small "whatever" box for filing all the things that deserve to be ignored. The greatest blessing a person could possibly receive in the brains department would be a *bottomless* "whatever" box: politics, economics, Social Security, illegal immigration, partisan corruption, steroids in sports, must-see TV, Donald Trump, Joe Biden, the IRS, the Middle East, hell, the future itself … whatever. I gots to fry me up this here bologna sandwich.

A writer's mind usually refuses to shut down. It pushes for more understanding, more insight, more truth, more humor, more whatever—in the case of Einstein, more really, really confusing math. Some creative people are good at dealing with this bombardment of ideas (Einstein), and others … well, Hunter S. Thompson comes to mind as a pretty good example of the road less traveled successfully. In my case, my demise came about *not* as a result of any great level of unsustainable brilliance, but because of an inability to square my McTalents with my particular profession. As an advertising guy, I found that things just reached the point where I could no longer spend a whole day working on an idea, pitch it to a client, and after *one second* of deliberation hear them say, "Well, what about if … ?"

The problem was me, not them. My brain snapped, crackled, and popped.

And so I quit the advertising business—told my boss it was time to vamoose, put my stuff in a banker's box, and drove home. No severance, no prospects, and probably no wife when she found out.

I sat around in a daze for a couple weeks, and then …
I had an idea! Phone-call time:

ME: Hey, man. It's me.

AGENT: Prioleau! What's up?

ME: I've got an idea for a book.

AGENT: I'm all atwitter.

ME: I quit my job.

AGENT: Good start.

ME: I don't have another job lined up.

AGENT: Ah, you're going for *The Razor's Edge* thing here? A novel?

ME: No, dude. That's not the pitch. It's a fact.

AGENT: You mean you actually quit your job … as in, you quit your job and have no paycheck?

ME: Correct.

AGENT: Prioleau, you've got to earn me some money before you call up looking to borrow some.

ME: No, no, no. Here's my idea: It's a book called *You Want Fries With That?* And it's a memoir about a white-collar burnout dropping out of the rat race and working minimum-wage jobs.

AGENT: Man. I actually like it. I really like it. How much have you gotten done?

ME: This phone call.

AGENT: Well, lemme see it when it's done.

ME: Can you sell it?

AGENT: I'll know after I read it.

ME: Dude, dude, dude—you've read my stuff. You know it's good. Can you sell it, you know, like, on spec? Get someone to agree to it before I actually work these jobs? I read that most nonfiction books are bought based on an outline.

AGENT: That's true ... when it's an expert writing on a topic within their expertise. A renowned motivational speaker writing a rah-rah book. A doctor writing about health. A CEO writing about management. Or an author with a successful book about George Washington under his belt, who says he wants to do one on Jefferson. Does that sound like you?

ME: I'm a good writer.

AGENT: Did I miss something in your resumé that qualifies you as an expert in the field of minimum-wage jobs? Do you have a massive following on social media begging you to post your next commentary on minimum-wage jobs? Do you have a bestselling book out there I don't know about? Unless one of those things is true, you're gonna have to actually write the book before I can sell it.

I cracked my first beer early that day.

LIVING THE DREAM

It's Not a Vacation When You're Unemployed. ...

Quitting your white-collar job to seek the publishing grail feels great. You can drink on weeknights, sleep late, then pad around the house saying to yourself, "Well. This is the life of a writer. I know, because I'm a writer."

What writer doesn't dream about the blessing of writing full-time? My guess would be that 90 percent of the writers reading these words practice their craft after work, when they could be watching Netflix or going out with friends. Once the brain starts buzzing, a writer can't *not* write. I felt a bit high, just reveling in my good fortune.

The high lasted until the first bill arrived. Hello, home insurance. It wasn't a killer or anything—we had plenty of money saved and invested—but it did tickle an itch in the back of my mind, which said, "Day Seven as a writer ... two thousand dollars out, and zero dollars in."

Hmmm.

Three weeks later, a similar epiphany struck as the monthly bills screamed for nourishment, but this time, the voice said, "Day Thirty as a writer ... seven thousand four hundred dollars out, and zero dollars in."

Writer's high, meet writer's horror. The checkbook was bleeding money like Johnny Depp planning his birthday party, and not a bloody cent came in to replace it. It was time to get going on those minimum-wage jobs and start writing.

A "Good Idea" Doesn't Mean a "Fun Idea"

The more I pondered my idea for the book, the better it seemed. Who among us doesn't have gut-wrenching stories from some awful job back in our salad days? Who doesn't chuckle when friends share their tales of working the fast-food fry station? How many laughs have been shared when friends get on the topic of the worst job they ever had?

The problem with my idea, however, was the *reality* of it: I was actually going to have to work these jobs. Not shadow an employee for a day or chat with someone about what it's like. No, no. I had to go apply, get hired, and actually show up for work. Can you, my friend, picture yourself at age fifty, adorned in a Burger World visor and nametag? How about ringing a doorbell and handing someone you know their pizza? At age fifty? Can't envision it? I couldn't, either.

The other reality that hit me involved a merger of physics and economics: As nature abhors a vacuum, so capitalism abhors a checking account. And as nature will destroy a vacuum, so the free market destroyed my checking account. After working the appropriate mathematical formulas based on minimum-wage paychecks, an obvious conclusion emerged: I could cover our bills working these jobs, provided I skipped lunch and only slept four hours every three weeks. Begrudgingly, I put the word out to my marketing contacts on the street that I was available for freelance and consulting projects.

Over the next year, my W-2 form boasted paychecks from such career endeavors as pizza delivery guy, ice-cream scooper, construction worker, ER tech, wrangler on a dude-ranch wagon train, and a big, fat zero that came from an extensive but failed attempt to get hired on by two of the big-box retailers. I absolutely reveled in making fun of the franchise policies, moronic/greedy owners, rude and obnoxious customers, and the absurdities of the situations, but I confess that it was very distressing to see up close the wonderful people who were trapped in these dead-end jobs.

Wealthy people love to express moral outrage over the unfairness that some Americans spend their lives trapped as minimum-wage workers, but it's just virtue signaling—and hollow virtue signaling at that. I don't see them tipping the guy at the Zippy Mart, giving hundred-dollar tips to the pizza man, insisting that all the waitstaff at their lavishly catered parties be paid fifty dollars an hour, or stopping by while their next mansion is being built to deliver extra cash to the laborers at the construction site. If by some million-to-one chance you're one of those "so concerned" virtue signalers and happen to be reading this, either shut up or start making it rain with tips, all day, to everyone who serves you.

Finally, a Decent Phone Call

Anyway, the sum total of the madness yielded a manuscript I felt proud of, which I immediately overnighted to my agent. A week later, the phone rang.

AGENT: Prioleau, I love it. That's the good news. The bad news is … well, you know the bad news. It's lacking the most important chapter of all.

ME: I was hoping you wouldn't notice that.

AGENT: You proposed a book called *You Want Fries With That?* and submitted a manuscript where you haven't worked for a fast-food joint.

ME: Oh, yeah—I think a better title will be *The Pizza Man Cometh.*

AGENT: The freaking name of the book is *You Want Fries With That?* It's a little obvious you failed to represent in that particular profession.

Me: Dude.

Agent: Keep it real. Send me the pages when you've done it.

With the same enthusiasm the slaves used to stack stones for the pharaoh, yours truly waded into the hamburger combat zone and landed a job. Let me tell you: Getting a job at one of those joints is way more difficult than you think—not because the qualifications are tough, but because the managers are either overworked, brain dead, or achieved the Peter Principle back when the previous manager put them in charge of the French fry station. Applications bearing my name languished at *nine* national chains before I finally confronted a manager by pointing out that I had submitted my application three days earlier, and *since then* they'd put out a new Help Wanted sign.

"Oh," she said. "Okay. You're hired."

The job yielded the pages, and the pages yielded a finished manuscript. Bring on the fame!

A couple of weeks later, my agent called.

"You use the word *I* too much. It's boring. *I* did this, *I* did that. You've got to hack those out."

"The book is about *me* doing this and *me* doing that," I replied. "How the hell do I explain something *I* did without using the word *I*?"

"They don't *all* have to come out. Just, like, ninety percent."

"I repeat my previous question."

"And I repeat my previous request. And since I'm selling the book, it's probably a good idea for you to figure it out."

Verbs That Don't Fight Back

The space above represents the weeks spent eliminating the word *I* from my manuscript. Oh, and if you would, please take an admiring moment to notice the paucity of *I*s in this manuscript, despite the fact this book, too, is about "me" doing this and "me" doing that. How did *I* do it? *I* don't know.

Anyway, the revised manuscript flew north. Fast-forward a month.

"You've got to get rid of all these passive verbs," my agent told me.

"Good lord. How do you write a sentence without using frickin' verbs?"

"*Passive* verbs, ya dolt."

"What in the hell is a passive verb? A verb that doesn't fight back?"

"Google it. Learn it. Fix it."

The space above represents the month I needed to research and understand active versus passive verbs, then decide to go *Texas Chainsaw* on my agent, then change my mind due to my fear of reentering the submission process at step one, then rewrite the freakin' manuscript. It was an exercise in mental torture. Or perhaps I should say, *The exercise tortured me mentally.* Yet another manuscript flew north, and I figured that if my book outsold the Bible for two straight years, an average hourly return of minimum wage might be attainable for all the work I'd already done on it.

Upon receiving the newly morphed manuscript, my agent called to shower me with praise. "Damn," he said. "I can sell this."

BEST CALL EVER

I was sitting on my porch the following month when my cell phone announced an incoming call with the sweet, sweet opening chords from the Auburn Fight Song. I took the call.

"Who's the best freakin' agent in the world?" the caller asked.

And, man, I *knew*. Knew who it was, knew why he was calling, and knew for sure my wife had bought a case of beer the night before. A cold one was in my hand and half-gone before I could shout the words, "You, baby, you!"

And that was that.

My agent had sold my book ... sold it to a real, live, New York publishing house. Whether that meant I got paid or screwed-blued-and-tattooed was anyone's guess, but one thing was a reality: A brief moment in recorded history now existed when someone on the planet who knew good writing had read my work and said, "You, sir, do not suck." The future may hold riches, fame, and a Nobel/Pulitzer combo, but for this writer, they will all pale in comparison to that evening on the porch.

Around midnight, while still on the porch drinking beer, a fleeting memory of a doctor's appointment the following morning clawed its way through the dead and dying brain cells to the tiny part of my brain assigned to "important issues." I called the medical office phone number to cancel, but it wouldn't take a message. To my horror, my phone rang two minutes later, and the caller announced himself as "Doctor Something."

"Doc," I said, "no can do on my appointment in the morning."

"Is something wrong?" he asked.

"Negative, doc," I responded. "I just sold a book, and—dude, I am *way* hammered!"

Neither he nor my wife found my comment funny, but I thought it showed creativity in a no-win situation.

Pithy notes should've been jotted down over the next few days, but stupid-happy thoughts clouded my thinking. Truth be told, the victory buzz sort of overwhelmed me, and even led me to tell a couple of potential marketing clients that business was booming, and that "my firm" (me) wasn't taking on any new work. Part of this statement was true—because getting loaded every night and sleeping until noon *does* make it hard to take on new projects.

Although I'm loath to admit it, fantasies of "author riches" began to slither around my brain. Like most struggling writers, I'd never considered the money … validation is what we crave the most. But still, thoughts of being a bestseller danced like sugarplums in my head, bouncing and ricocheting and wrecking all intelligent thought. Thinking about the public actually reading my work ran neck and neck with the thought of buying a new boat and calling it *Write On*.

After a week, the buzz started to fade, so I called my agent.

ME: What do you hear?

AGENT: All good news. They're going to release you in their spring catalog, which is really fast. Should be April.

ME: Umm, it's only August, dude.

AGENT: I know. April is practically tomorrow in publishing time.

ME: Wow … I guess I better get serious about cranking up my consulting business. How long before writing could serve as a sustainable career?

AGENT: How about never? How does never fit into your schedule?

ME: Seriously, is being a full-time writer something that might work out?

AGENT: You really don't know, do you?

ME: Sounds like some reality is fixin' to get crammed up my nose.

AGENT: There are about a hundred writers in these United States who actually make a no-kidding living as an author. The other full-time authors come from money, or married money. The odds of you becoming a full-time, no-other-job author are about the same as taking up golf and playing in the Master's next year.

ME: You're telling me something here, I think.

AGENT: Yes, that's true. What do you suppose it is?

ME: I need to get a job and go back to writing after work?

AGENT: We're making progress.

A few days later, the first email from my publisher arrived. My publisher. My publisher. My publisher. My publisher. My ... uh, sorry. Anyway, the email read as very kind and complimentary, welcoming me into the family. It explained that there would be a contract arriving shortly, and that my job entailed signing it and returning three copies to them. I called my agent to find out what to do.

"If I were you," he said, "I'd sign it."

What's That in Dog Years?

All right! With a publisher on board and a couple of maxed-out credit cards, I began to feel like a real artist:

broke, with no means of reliable income, and clueless about my future. It felt so right. In the zone. A few months of ramen noodles, and genuine starving artist status could be mine.

Here's a brief look at the questions I thought would soon be proactively answered by my publisher:

1. Will I make any money?
2. Will there be a book tour?
3. Will my expenses on the book tour be covered?
4. What will the cover of my book look like?
5. What are my promotional responsibilities, and what are the publisher's?
6. What should I be doing to prepare for this experience?
7. Should I be working on another book?
8. What should the follow-up book be about?
9. What *is* the frequency, Kenneth?

Here's the total number of those questions they addressed: 0.

I should've been a big boy and just asked, but I was worried. What if my questions offended my new overlords? What if I spoke out of turn? Insulted their professionalism? Asked something stupid? I liken it to crawling through the desert, dying of thirst, and someone comes along on a camel and offers you a diet cola. I loathe diet cola. I cannot put into words how much I hate it. Should I ask for water and take the chance he'll be insulted and trot away to help someone who's more appreciative?

That terror muted my tongue, and because none of these topics ever came up, I thought they'd be addressed down the road. So I avoided asking anything stupid—which was stupid.

The Hollywood Dream

The section you are reading at the moment was added as part of the rewrite process. Why? Because it's important to come clean on my stupidity in the early going. Not only were the questions above unanswered, but the only thing I knew about publishing revolved around what you see in the movies. Every writer watches these movies, and based on my intake of data, here's what I assumed would happen:

Viewing me as an up-and-comer, my publisher would do whatever they could to "groom" my talent, and ensure that I remained part of their stable of writers for years to come.

The publisher would fly me first-class to New York so I could meet the team, as surely everyone in the building would want to get a feel for this new writer they "signed" and say a few things like, "Huge fan of your work. Huge. Lotta buzz on the streets. My brother is a wealth management consultant—here's his card. You'll need him."

Having inspected the cut of my jib, the publisher would select an editor to work with me ... an editor they thought would "bring out the best in me," but one with a light touch; everyone knows you don't ruffle the feathers of a genius.

Someone at the publishing house would have an extended sit-down with me and discuss the importance of watching out for other publishers making huge financial offers for my next book.

While the book went through the steps toward getting published, the publishing house would hire entire shifts of PR pros to tirelessly "work the streets," talking with everyone from book clubs to the CEO of Barnes & Noble. It wouldn't be long before they had even the performance artists in SoHo atwitter about the upcoming release.

A team of specialists at the publishing house would discuss the book, look at publishing industry trends, and offer insights on the topics I should consider (as quickly as possible) for my next book. They'd say things like, "The next Harry Potter sequel drops on the first of May next year. We need to be in play the day before, because your sequel will likely suck the wind outta those sails."

The day the book launched, we'd find the CEO and CFO of the company alone in the building, drinking whiskey neat, monitoring sales, and discussing the fact my book could "launch an entirely new market in the industry."

Oh, and I thought celestial choirs would descend on the backs of unicorns, a white dove would land on my shoulder, and the voice of James Earl Jones would announce to the four corners of the Earth: "This is my author, with whom I am well pleased."

Here's how many of these things happened: zero.

Could Hollywood have misled me? Would they paint an unrealistic picture of the life of an author? Had they made it look cool and exciting, just to sell tickets to their movies?

No way. Not Hollywood.

Yes, Hollywood.

But, I learned, such is the nature of being signed by a big publishing house. The truth is, I represented a one-kilobyte file, in a thousand-terabyte mainframe. And, as would soon become apparent, a book is only going to succeed based on exceptional content, tireless marketing by the author, and a lucky break. A very lucky break.

Side note about another "hole in my publishing knowledge": Although the major publishers no longer have the time or manpower to provide the "Hollywood" version of working with authors, there are smaller publishers who do exactly that—in fact, many of them are like you and me, and practice their craft because they love it ... not to comb through thousands of manuscripts looking for the next Harry Potter, but to groom talent that may produce the next J. K. Rowling.

Whether the CEO stays up the night of the launch drinking whiskey and counting sales remains unknown to me, but it would be cool, no?

If you can find a small publishing house to take a look at your work, do it. Remember, however: A small publishing house puts a great deal at risk—time and money they may not have—when they take on a new writer. As I said earlier, send them work that's soaked in your blood, sweat, and tears.

So, gentle reader, if you're seeking a big publishing house, there's some lessons for you to take to the bank, because odds are you won't be taking many royalty checks there.

1. Ask questions.
2. Don't expect much.
3. If you start to expect much more than not much, remind yourself that you read this book, which obviously you didn't get much out of.
4. Until you're selling a hundred thousand copies each time you publish something new, the "thank you" you'll get from the publisher is whatever royalty checks you receive. You see, the big publishing house is just a business ... and businesses view their monetary investment as a much bigger deal than your silly typing. They think *you* should be thanking *them*, until such time as you're so big, you might move on to another big publisher. When that happens? Tell them to send all communications to you with an enclosed self-addressed, stamped envelope.

WAIT, WHAT'S HAPPENING HERE?

Just about the time I thought the postal service had lost my career in a package mix-up, an email arrived informing me that "step one" would be reformatting my manuscript—essentially, transforming my initial mess into something the copy editor could work with. I think a good translation might be: "The Word document you originally submitted was a complete disaster, and you need to fix it."

It struck me as odd that I, a soon-to-be famous literary author (peace be upon my name), would be asked to reformat my manuscript. In accordance with my very effective strategy at the time, I didn't bother to ask questions. And I didn't say, "If I knew how to format it, it wouldn't have been a mess, would it?" So I paid someone to do it.

When I asked the publisher of the book you're reading if I'd have to find someone to reformat my Word doc for *this* book, she laughed and said, "Of course not. What kind of Mickey Mouse outfit would ask the writer to do the technical work?"

"Big ones," is what I didn't say.

The note about my need to reformat the mess said that the manuscript would be arriving shortly—and it needed only minimal reformatting work: In fact, the publisher stated, most of the editing symbols would be familiar to me from my days in advertising. Exciting stuff, and doubly so, since a new query had materialized for me to add to my list of questions—namely, "What the hell is a copy editor?"

When the manuscript arrived, I opened it with a certain smug satisfaction, my mastery of Word having been so tight that the formatting would be "minimal." Flipping through the pages, my smugness melted away, and I wondered if my publisher actually knew the definition of the word *minimal*. The pages bore only a slight resemblance to the document I had submitted. Virtually every paragraph had a "format editing" mark on it, and the end result looked like some sort of hieroglyphic translation of the Dead Sea Scrolls. I thumbed through the pages carefully, and not so much as an inkling on how to reformat the mess came to mind.

Yes, it felt good to see that not many words were changed, but this formatting thing fit into my wheelhouse the way public speaking fits into Joe Biden's.

Stymied, the former Marine in me stepped in to take control: I emailed my publisher and said, "Got the manuscript. No problem. Have it back to you in two weeks."

My "no problem" scheme entailed hiring a former colleague-savant to enter the jungle of dashes, indents, returns, and alignments, which she hacked through over the next two weeks. Although she deserved every cent I paid her, she did, of course, send an invoice. Your favorite soon-to-be author already appeared to be losing money on this endeavor. My subconscious whispered to me the words that ruled much of my life: "Hey, dude ... you're doing it wrong."

Speaking of Doing It Wrong ...

Over the years, I had studied and dissected a number of interviews with successful writers, hoping to glean some insight into how to achieve publication. A number of these writers expressed dissatisfaction with the cover art assigned to their books and lamented the fact that creative control of the cover lay exclusively with the publisher. My response? Boo-hoo-hoo, ya spoiled, egotistical jerk. You're *published*. Shut up, be happy, and revel in the victory. I made a solemn vow that should a publishing break ever drop into my lap, I'd be the "coolest" author ever, and be entirely gracious about any decisions my publisher made.

When the initial cover for my book arrived, one thing occurred to me: No jury in the world would convict me for the violence I was contemplating. The unknown graphic designer quickly became the target of an assassination plot swirling in my head. Fortunately, my phone rang.

AGENT: Dude, I just got the cover. When it comes in, don't look at it. Delete it.

ME: Too late.

AGENT: Okay, we can work through this. We need to use respectful *persuasion*, okay? Whatever you do, don't be going all Elton John on me.

ME: It's not a problem, boss.

AGENT: You *like* it?

ME: No, but after the designer goes missing, we'll get a new design team assigned to redo the cover.

AGENT: Seriously, man. Be cool. It's just an initial concept. These guys are total pros, and they'll come up with something great. Just be patient.

ME: Bro, did you see that thing? Steps must be taken. It's like the law of the jungle, where certain sacrifices must be made for the good of the herd. Joe Antelope doesn't want his bow-legged son to get eaten by the crocodiles, but the herd must thrive. I'll be thinning a weak link from the graphic-design herd.

AGENT: Pretty good analogy, actually.

ME: I'm not throwing a tantrum here ... just saying.

AGENT: Look, we just need to give them some better ideas to latch onto.

ME: Okay, here's an idea: The designer goes missing.

AGENT: Look, you're a writer. *And* you come up with spiffy ideas as a profession. Just combine the two and win them over.

ME: Aren't you supposed to do this stuff? What do I pay you for?

AGENT: How much have you been paid so far?

ME: Nothing.

AGENT: Right. And fifteen percent of nothin' is nothin'.

Soldier of Misfortune

With all the waiting built into the process, life demanded a varsity effort on my part to keep from going (further) broke. Hanging on until the publication of my book was paramount, at which point (a) it would sell, and I'd be a groovy writer guy making a living, or (b) it wouldn't sell, and I could blame all my life's problems on my broken heart, spiral out of control, burn down my house, and wander the streets of my hometown muttering. I would offer the tortured-artist defense to all who inquired, and the world at large would give me a mulligan. But what to do now? For money?

Sadly, my chosen career path offered only one real skill: marketing. Yes, as a former Marine officer, I could join a mercenary outfit like Blackwater and generate some decent coin protecting dignitaries, but when I inquired about employment with Blackwater, they asked how many miles I still ran per week.

"Mile … sss? As in plural?" I responded.

So, marketing it would have to be. And thus, Little Fish Consulting was born.

Back to laying stones for the pharaoh.

Working Virtual Before Virtual Was Cool

As consulting jobs began coming in, both my wife and I found ourselves working out of our home. Office space costs money, and since we didn't have any, the home-office solution carried the day. A husband and a wife both working out of the home can be difficult, however, especially if the man makes his living doing something subjective, like writing.

Should you ever have the opportunity to "write full-time" and find yourself working at home with your significant other, here are a few notes on the inherent challenges:

1. No matter what you're writing—the great American novel, a brochure, an ad campaign, a freelance

magazine article, or a piece for the church bulletin—there is one rock-solid constant: You are sitting at a computer doing it.

2. Here are some optional things you do at the computer: Waste time on the web, forward stupid emails, and google terms like *John Wick* and *fight scenes*.

3. If you compose Pulitzer Prize–level literature for six straight hours, then take three minutes to watch a funny video on Facebook, an infallible law within the space-time continuum ensures that your wife will walk up behind you during those three minutes.

4. Once this phenomenon has occurred more than once, which it must do under the aforementioned universal laws, your wife will swear before her creator that your writing-to-screwing-off ratio is, at best, one part writing for every nine parts screwing off. This fact will embed itself into her brain, and remain there with a clarity normally reserved for unkind things you said a decade ago.

NOTE: IMPORTANT DATA BELOW:

5. As discussed so brilliantly in the book *Men Are from Mars, Women Are from Venus*, men are from Mars and women are from Venus. A man compartmentalizes data, "hunts" down solutions, and leans into tasks until they are either complete or he is exhausted. A woman, on the other hand, is

a stream-of-consciousness thinker, "gathers" ideas, and has the ability to mentally multitask hundreds of to-do lists simultaneously.

6. Once your wife "feels" you are goofing off over there on the computer, she will inject her Venusian style of thinking into your Martian world, and her stream-of-consciousness thinking will gush forth whenever an available second arises. Example: She's on the phone with a client, and you are desperately trying to strangle out of your brain a word that rhymes with *orange*. Her client puts her on hold. Suddenly, she has a free moment for streaming thoughts:

You: Orange. Borange? Corange? Dorange?

Her: Hey, sweetie, did you remember to call your great-grandmother and thank her for sending us that article "Better Sex for Married Couples"?

You: Forange? Gorange? No, I'll do it tonight.

Her: I asked you yesterday.

You: Zorange? I'm working.

Her: (With telepathic smirk) Ahh. Well, please call her before you forget.

You: Horange? Morange?

Her: *Please.* Now. While you're thinking about it?

You: I'll do it, hon.

HER: Good. Right now. Oh, and while you're up, can you take the trash out, walk the dog, email our Bible study group about Wednesday, and rescreen the porch? And don't forget—(caller on phone interrupts her)—Oh, hey, Janet. No problem. Do you need me to stop over and discuss the options?

YOU: Please, Janet! Say you need her over there now! Demand that she come! I'm frickin' beggin' you!

Though it's true that this type of banter doesn't lead to an evening of champagne and *amore*, it does have an upside: By the time the silence in your home office lifts, you will have had ample time to find a word that rhymes with *orange*. Probably a word that rhymes with *purple*, too.

Makin' Copies

The next step revealed to me in the publishing process involved the "copy editor," a job distinctly different from that of whoever did the formatting stuff. As you may recall from an earlier comment, the copy editor's role mystified me, but I acted informed when my publisher emailed to tell me the "copy-edited manuscript" was on its way. Fortunately, the manuscript arrived with a letter explaining the copy editor's job:

a. They search out questionable issues regarding time, continuity, and language.

b. They flag things the writer needs to confirm.

c.   They cover the manuscript with strange symbols that provide direction to the person typesetting the book into its final form.

d.   They provide guidance in areas where your wording is confusing, where you've repeated analogies, and spots where you slipped into general suckage.

Upon its arrival, I looked the manuscript over, and it occurred to me that the copy editor deserved to make more money than me, my agent, and the publisher combined. He, for instance, pointed out that "Rubik's Cube" served as an analogy on page 78, and asked if it shouldn't perhaps be changed to another concept when it appeared again on page 203. He found a few continuity errors. He noted my excessive use of the words *heaving breasts*. He even reviewed my permanent record and noticed some holes in the defense I'd mounted in kindergarten when I was (falsely) accused of eating paste.

I was, however, thrilled at how little of my actual prose he'd changed. Most authors I've talked to, even very successful ones, told me the editing and rewriting process was so painful, they felt like they were giving birth. Needless to say, I felt quite proud of myself.

I called my friend/novelist Beth and asked about her copy editor. She told me her editor noticed that a cat in her novel was pregnant two weeks longer than it should have been. People, this isn't a skill … this is unrewarded genius. In addition to his ability to cross-reference and retain facts like Bobby Fischer, my copy editor also painted the entire manuscript in a maze of markings, lines, and squiggles whose meaning was surely known only to him, the typesetter, and the handful of Middle Earth wizards who developed them.

It took me a while to understand why the process of reviewing the copy editor's notes felt so pleasurable. After all, who enjoys working on something they've already worked on? Worked on, like, twenty times? Then, once again, Colonel Kurtz's diamond bullet hit me between the eyes: The copy editor, and by extension, the publisher, was asking *me* if I wanted to change something ... *if* a particular phrase could be improved ... *if* a particular reference would make sense to the readers.

Only an advertising writer can connect with the sublime ecstasy of this experience. Understand, dear friend, that just a year earlier, my writing was being judged and rewritten by car dealers and the like. These yo-yos—who couldn't write a coherent sentence with a shotgun duct-taped to their head—read my stuff ... in front of me ... for the first time ... *with a red pen in their hand*. Even worse, some fancied themselves "just too busy," and dispatched their *secretary* to review and edit my copy. The process was a day-after-day kick in the crotch, as my professional skills were devalued to the point of mockery.

It was at that moment, holding my marked-up, copy-edited manuscript in one hand, that I stood atop a mountain of joy and flipped a furious bird to copy-tweaking advertising clients all over the world, proclaiming, "Eat meeeeeeeeeeeeeee!"

Though I knew I might *never* get another book published, for one sweet, shining moment in time, I stood on the victory platform, and my banner ran up the flagpole as the band played "God Bless America."

Celebrities Sucking

As more weeks ticked by and I launched into writing the book you're reading right now, I pondered the reason: "Why?" Why write a book about having written a book? I came up with a twofold answer.

First, to let the wonderful people who actually spend their hard-earned money on *books* understand what a first-time author experiences; second, to reach out to all my brothers-and-sisters-in-typing clawing their way toward publication and say, "I feel your pain." Not rehearsed, Bill Clinton–style, bite-my-lip pain, but your *real* pain … bad-hangover-from-MD-20/20-with-a-hatchet-in-your-head pain.

Some of that pain—a particularly sharp, stabbing pain—is the fact that many members of the book-buying public choose to purchase books written by celebrities. Because people buy them, big publishers print them. After all, they're in the business of making money, not validating dreamers' dreams.

As a result, celebrities are everywhere, sucking up way more than their share of the available publishing oxygen.

Children's books, novels, autobiographies, cookbooks—you name the genre, and celebrities are lining up with their hands out. Many of them receive obscene advances for books they don't write a word of. In fact, many of them confess to meeting with their designated ghostwriter (aka sellout scrivener) no more than a handful of times. Do ya think maybe, just maybe, a ghostwriter wrote the book "by" James Patterson and Bill Clinton? Given that the "novel" centered around the kidnapping of the First Lady, maybe they came up with it when ol' James asked Bill, "If you could wish for one thing, what would it be?" But I'd hazard a guess that neither involved themselves in any way beyond that.

Here's a very, very brief list of some of the giants of literature who have managed to secure publication: Paris Hilton. Britney Spears. Pamela Anderson. Suzanne Somers. Loni Anderson. Tori Spelling. Madonna. Victoria Beckham. And those, friend, are merely the *female* "authors" who popped up when I googled "Famous blond females who would be slinging hash at IHOP if they had a size A cup, but instead are both insanely rich AND have somehow gotten their names listed on the cover of a book as the author."

Look, I've got no problem with comedians, lawyers, and multitalented geniuses like the late Michael Crichton writing books, because writing is largely what they do for a living. But Pam Anderson? Paris Hilton? Perhaps I'm a bit of a snob, but … no, I'm not. This is frickin' publishing, damnit. This is the written word, professionally printed on paper by an offset press. If a tree is going to die, shouldn't *toilet paper* be its most embarrassing possible fate?

Big publishing's investment in celebrity authors has even spawned a theater comedy named, well, *Celebrity Autobiography*, where comedians will sit on an empty stage and read directly from such autobiographies. One review of a performance stated, "I laughed so hard, I truly thought I was going to pee my pants." And all these comedians are doing is reading exact excerpts from celebrities' books.

That, my nonwriting friends, is painful for an aspiring author to even know about, much less see when they enter a bookstore.

The Typeset Pages

My manuscript arrived for the third and final time, and it looked like the actual pages of a book. It was awesome. It had all these cool registration marks, and the individual lines were numbered, and there was that groovy little touch where they put the name of the book at the top of a page, and the name of the chapter on the other. It looked like a damn book!

The joy of the moment dissipated when I began reading it—again—for the zillionth time. My baby no longer made me laugh. We were now like an eighty-year-old couple—sure, we had fond memories to share, but our encounter tonight certainly wasn't going to lead to any thunder down under. I worked my way through it, found a couple of typos, and emailed them to the publisher.

Blurb? What the Hell Is a Blurb?

About that time, a message from my agent pinged me, and we began an email exchange:

AGENT: Publisher wants to know who you know that's in the biz ... preferably famous.

ME: I know a few famous people. Why?

AGENT: They need someone to write a blurb about your book for the catalog and the book cover.

ME: Okay. How many?

AGENT: If you know someone, contact them.

ME: Dude, is this something you should be doing as my agent?

AGENT: No.

Somebody? Hey, It's Me, Nobody

Once again, another challenge surfaced for me, the first-time author: I was in charge of tracking down people to write glowing, witty things about my book. Is this normal? Hell, your own mom doesn't even want to read your manuscript. It's ugly and looks like a PhD dissertation. And I doubt some brilliant author emerging from the hollers of West Virginia would know anyone famous.

I pondered the people I'd mentioned … and thus the stalking began. I hunted each of them down via friends, family, and Google, and then, well, I begged. I begged like Dubya in front of the Yale admissions board … like Johnny Depp forty-five minutes after last call … like Bill bowing before Hillary when the DNA tests on Monica's dress came back … like a canceled celebrity trying to win back the raging mob of trolls … like the CEO of Haliburton in a war-extension meeting with the Secretary of Defense. I don't think anyone has begged that hard since Pete Davidson found out Kim Kardashian was dumping him.

Mercifully, one by one, they relented. I sent out manuscripts, and some sent back blurbs. One of my proudest moments in life came when Pat Conroy (a family friend) described my book as "magnificent."

Of course, the *inside* secret is that it didn't matter what they wrote—all we needed was their name on an email with some words in it. Let's hypothetically say my friend Mr. Big wrote a blurb that said, "Throughout the book, Prioleau Alexander tries to be funny, but he's not. His writing is terrible, and his suppositions are outrageous. I laughed out loud maybe once, and that was at how poorly he bumbled his descriptions. I'd recommend this book to anyone who likes wasting money, time, and brain power. Otherwise, forget it. Grade: F. Someone should hack off Mr. Alexander's fingers."

Gee, Mr. Big, thanks! We can use it!

"Funny ... outrageous ... I laughed out loud ...
I'd recommend this book to anyone. ... "

—*Mr. Big*

Did we actually do that sort of selective editing on my book? Fortunately, no. But now that I know about it, I understand perfectly how they get "good reviews" for lousy movies.

THE TIMES, THEY ARE A' CHANGING?

You Gotta Ask Yourself a Question: Do I Feel Lucky?

As I've mentioned, the pace at which the publishing industry moves is glacial. Having come from the advertising industry, where everything is a cliff-hanging emergency, the whole process felt like a root canal in a time warp. I'm now in the club, so let's *go*! Give me another topic, agree in advance to publish it, and I'll write a book about it. Send me to Afghanistan. Send me to the presidential debates. Send me backstage on *American Idol*. Hell, send me to San Francisco, where I'll write an exposé entitled "How the Crown Jewel of the Golden State Came to Have City Employees Who Are Literally Paid to Clean Up Human

Crap." Send me *somewhere*, let me make fun of someone who needs it, and let's get something accomplished!

As if by divine providence, an email arrived from my agent. This was fortunate for both of us, because I was about to start bugging him, and … well, we all know what a sweetheart he was to begin with:

P,

> *Time for a rewrite on your humorous history book. Your ridiculous overuse of ellipses and passive verbs must be addressed. We might get lucky and sell it as a follow-up to* Fries.

I replied:

Dude,

> *I'm all over it. Any specific thoughts or direction? I know the humorous parts can be improved, and the pop-culture references can be updated, and converting the verbs sounds like a real party. What else?*

His answer:

> *Sorry. After getting your note I reread my email, and I now see my failure to utilize sufficient pronouns. Let me further clarify. I, the agent, want YOU, the writer, to do the rewrite. The*

word we *referred to getting lucky and selling it. Sorry for the confusion.*

My sweet agent's bedside manner aside, this was the exact distraction I needed. My writing-to-screwing-off ratio was getting out of kilter, and my bride began to suspect that she and I had different definitions of *full-time*. Every evening after work for four months, I edited and converted verbs and generally worked to update things. I'd morphed into a more polished wordsmith over the years, and thus applied all my new tricks of the trade to the manuscript. All that toil resulted in a work I felt offered more fun per page than the book I currently had in the pipeline to publication. I couldn't wait until my agent saw it! Our "best friends forever" status would come to fruition yet!

A Clear and Present Danger

About this time in the process, I found myself talking over beers with a good friend who ain't been right since Al Gore invented the internet. You probably know the type: the guy who can no longer accept anyone else's advice on anything electronic, because the ability to do research via the web has enlightened them with an angry expertise. Anyway, during our conversation, I mentioned that my first book would hit the streets in the spring, and he looked at me like I'd just bragged about my new video game, Donkey Kong.

"Why would you mess with an old-economy publishing company? You should be blogging."

This took me aback a little. My book now qualified as "old economy?" Who reads these things called blogs?

"A blog? How do you figure?"

"It's the twenty-first century, man. People don't have time for books. Blogs are the way for people of similar interest to connect. Like, if you're into photography, you can log onto a photography blog and find out what's up."

"Are these bloggers good writers?"

"It's about ideas, man. Not punctuation and grammar."

"Well, how do you know if the blog writer knows what he's talking about?"

"It's interactive. If he writes something wrong, you flame his ass."

"How does the blogger get paid?" I asked.

"That comes later. The web culture is about relationships, and you grow using those relationships."

"So this, uh, photography blog writer spends his own money and time to post his ideas on the web, but if he makes a mistake, guys like you are waiting to flame his ass."

"Exactly."

"Okay, one more thing. It sounds like the point of using blogs is to go to a blog about a topic you already know about. So what's the point? To insult someone from the safety of your own keyboard?"

"No, dawg. Blogs are the perfect way to learn about something new. Like, let's say—well, you don't know crap about technology, so let's pick an easy one: digital cameras. If you want to learn about them, you do a search for a blog on digital cameras."

"Okay, and when I get there, how do I know if the guy is an expert?"

"If he isn't, you'll see where people shoot him down."

"How do I know the people shooting him down are experts?"

"Dude, you ain't ready for blogs."

True statement, there. But, if people as bright as my friend thought a blog could encompass something as vast as "communications," I thought I should give it a look.

Before moving along, let me restate that the experiences explored in this book are from back in the days when comedians were allowed to tell jokes, looting and arson were considered crimes, and making out with a gal didn't require a contract stating that the make-out session was consensual, authorized, signed by both parties, and witnessed by a notary public. I just couldn't get my head around the idea of a blog, much in the same way I can't get my head around Twitter these days.

Sure, I understand the use of Twitter for announcing breaking news or for communications if you're a politician aiming to reach constituents ... but LeBron James? Who in the hell cares what a high school–educated basketball player thinks about international trade relations with China? Whoopi Goldberg letting me know it's "not the job" of a Catholic cardinal to decide who should get communion … when that is literally a part of the dude's job description? Let there be no doubt that I include nobodies like myself as part of the group that has no business on Twitter. What in the hell do we have to say in two sentences that anyone could possibly care about?

Anyway, per my buddy's suggestion, my first search demanded "Blog on Digital Cameras." Google returned 5.9 million websites, which, quite honestly, was a bit more information than I needed. I poked through a few of the sites listed on the first page, and it appeared that the blog, as a concept, had migrated a bit: Based on my buddy's description, I envisioned bloggers being writers who felt passionately about the topic of digital cameras and new digital photography techniques. Not so with digital cameras—it appeared that the freight train called capitalism had derailed that trend, and the HazMat crews hadn't even begun the cleanup. All the "digital camera blogs" I found were nothing more than professional product reviews, copy-and-pasted into websites that just so happened to sell the products being reviewed. I wondered if anyone had informed Inventor Gore that the previously socialist blog concept was drifting to the right.

I decided, however, against prematurely jumping to judgment concerning the almighty blog. Digital cameras are a product for sale, so it's quite natural for capitalism to elbow its way into the ring. I decided that to be fair to "the blog philosophy," I needed to search for some different topics. Specifically, *ideas*—after all, if my dream of paying the bills as a communicator of ideas was doomed from the outset because others were doing it for free, I wanted to know who these leftist book assassins were ... and if they could be stopped.

In order to be impartial, I did Google search number two, for "Blog on Minimum-Wage Jobs." This was the same topic that had yielded my first book deal, so it seemed like a good place to search. Google responded with more than 4.2 million hits. I felt pretty good, discovering that only 4.2 million other people were exploring the same general idea as I was. The rub, of course, lay in the question: "What do they have to say?"

I poked around and found a blog by a gentleman who opined on three of the minimum-wage jobs (from hell) he'd worked. Eureka! I'd found my competition. The average American "consumer of ideas" could purchase my ideas for $24.95, plus tax, or they could delve into this guy's blog for free. Hungrily, anxiously, I drilled down into the content, and discovered that he *did* have a way with words:

- "Minimum-wage jobs are exploitive to the tilt (*sic*)!"
- "I never saw so many smokers in my life!"
- "You are not appreciated for your work or your creativity."

I had to ask myself: Did my insights surpass these? Were my musings worth so much more money than the ever-seductive price of *free*? I pressed on, discovering a category within the topic he felt so passionately about that it generated the use of all caps:

- "Just about everybody who worked minimum-wage jobs had HORRIBLE ORAL HYGENE. I don't mean bad, I mean HORRIBLE. Broken and missing teeth, gingivitis was rampant, my only guess is that alcohol, tobacco, and poor diet along with a completely (*sic*) loss of hope of every (*sic*) achieving something in life had been made representational in their mouth. These people where (*sic*) branded for life, good luck getting a corporate job with a mouth that looks like it belongs in that of a wild animal!"

For the love of *Love in the Time of Cholera*, how can a *for-profit* writer compete for mind-share when *not-for-profit* writers are out there offering this level of material *free*?!! Insulting people who were trying to make a living, mocking their inability to afford braces, and criticizing their poor chances of obtaining a white-collar job? What insightful stuff!

As a final nail in my ego's coffin, the blogger hit me with his wrap-up, engaging his fellow thinkers on why minimum-wage jobs simply weren't for him:

- "Minimum-wage jobs and my personality just don't jive. I have no problem telling somebody that they are wrong, standing my ground and even telling them off if needed. I have a very direct managing method, no stories, good or bad, just tell me what is going on."

Based on reports that filter out about the current practices of corporate America, his "management" style will likely ensure his position as the CEO of General Electric before I finish dinner tonight.

Stunned and more than a little humbled, I searched again, this time for a blog on "turning thirty." As I've mentioned, the first manuscript I ever wrote followed this coming-of-age plotline, but it never made it to the publishing finish line. Perhaps the reason for my failure lay out there, in cyberspace, where a brilliant-but-free writer was covering the topic with greater humor, sensitivity, and insight. My "turning thirty" search yielded almost 2.2 million hits.

When undertaking a task like a coming-of-age memoir, even the boldest writer can be intimidated by the Shakespearean load of potential material. Here lies a topic that cries out for the unearthing of an underbelly of angst and optimism, regret and hope, naiveté and wisdom, light and dark, fear and loathing. *My* failure to achieve publication clearly indicated that I had failed in my quest, but what about these bloggers? Would their musings please the gods of rhetoric?

Here is one opening sentence that caught my eye:

> *Many females—especially if they're single and don't want to be, or they're in a relationship where they don't know where things are going, or if they haven't accomplished something in particular they wanted to do—look at the prospect of turning 30 and think they should have done something ... bigger ... than what they have.*

Dizzied, I lurched onward to another site:

> *I know persons twice my age who appear not to understand how anyone could possibly be disturbed at turning thirty.*

"Onward!" I cried. "Upward!"

I prepared to read the next page when a voice came from over my shoulder.

"Are you about to be mean? Your rule has always been to not make fun of individual people."

It was my much-better half, reminding me of the obvious. "But honey, these people are writing for public consumption. Some of them even have a banner on their site proclaiming, 'I support the Writers Guild of America on strike.' They need to be made fun of. They're crying out for it!"

"How do you figure? They're doing something they enjoy. They believe in themselves. Who are you to laugh at them?"

"Hon, suppose I wake up tomorrow and declare myself good-looking and buff? And I start taking pictures of myself in a Speedo, and posting the shots on the web? What would people do?"

"Puke?"

"Yeah, that, too, but they'd laugh at me, because I'm not a model, no matter how much I wish or think I am. These window lickers are drawing a solidarity reference between themselves and the Writers Guild. You don't get to call yourself a writer if you don't know what a double negative or a run-on sentence is. We can't have people out there, willy-nilly using the same words and language used by Shakespeare. It throws off the cosmic pecking order. Someone's gotta put a barrier to entry!"

"You're being mean-spirited, and it's beneath you."

Even as the words exited her mouth, I considered starting a blog about spouses who have no idea who they are actually married to, but thought better of it. Plus, she had made a good point—and you have to be married to know how overrated winning a debate with your wife can be.

Things Have Changed ... Even More

The blog, of course, is practically gone now, replaced by the podcast and TikTok and YouTube videos. Why?

Because blogs require (a) talent as a writer with a unique perspective on something relevant, and (b) users to actually read words, in an environment where reading is on its way to becoming as popular as using leeches for bloodletting.

Please read items (a) and (b) again. This is the art you are pursuing—an art that's vanishing faster than the career of a movie star who "comes out" as a Republican. If it's fame and fortune you seek, all signs point to TikTok as the new frontier. Maybe you could start a new "TikTok Challenge" where you see how many of your toes you can crush with a hammer without making a sound. Or you could create a new dance craze, where you smash the toes on one foot, then hop around on your uninjured foot in time with an oom-pah-pah song.

You must also remember that you're competing with some podcasters who have real talent. Yes, Harry Potter is second only to the Bible in book sales, but Joe Rogan's podcast likely has more ears in a year than Harry Potter's had eyeballs since day one.

Let's not forget, as well, there are like twenty premium cable channels streaming series as good as any movie you've ever seen. People simply don't need to seek entertainment anymore—it's shoved down their throats for $9.95 a month.

My point? Writing is hard. It takes discipline and practice. It requires you to read books and learn from other writers. For a writer, the only easy day was yesterday. Make sure the act of writing is what you love—not the dream at the end of the rainbow. At the end of the rainbow, there's a good chance you'll find not streets of gold, but a little dude named Oz, insisting that you ignore the little man behind the curtain.

The Lord Is, Indeed, Merciful

I wept with gratitude when the new cover design for my book arrived from the publisher. My tears of relief Gatlin-gunned out from my eyeballs, knocked my computer off the table, and scared my twelve-year-old mutt so bad, he pissed the rug. But I didn't care. My baby's cover no longer looked like Gollum's uglier brother. Sure, it didn't look like it possessed the shared DNA of Megan Fox and Ryan Gosling, either, but it was good enough for me to clean up dog pee with a smile on my face.

In my mind, the work was done: Agent sold the book. Book was edited and designed. Cover was done. I'd managed to find and submit an author photo where I didn't look completely like Shrek. Time to start talking about the next book, right? I mean, the process ain't that frickin' hard once you're in the club: Send manuscript to agent. Agent sells to publisher (with slam-dunk ease). Publisher reads, accepts, typesets, designs a cover—hell, the new book could conceivably come out on the very heels of my first book.

The final step was as easy as attaching the new manuscript to an email and crafting a note to my agent to sell him on my marketing insights:

Dude,

I finished the rewrite, and the manuscript is attached. I think you're going to be pleased. Since we're on track to publish Fries *in April, what do you think about pitching the publisher on the humorous history manuscript for an October release? This book lends itself to political discussion, and since October is a month when every radio and TV station is starving for political pundits, perhaps we could lie our way in the door, and pretend like I have a clue. That'd sell some books, no?*

A reply came back:

Please, seriously, get a job. Or a second job. Find something to do that distracts you from emailing me. But before you do, read your contract. There are some helpful hints in there.

To which I responded:

Dude,

I lost my copy of the contract. What do I need to know?

His reply:

> *First, you need to know that you are an idiot
> for losing your copy of the contract. Second, the
> publisher has sixty days after the publication of
> Fries to review your next book. That means that on
> day fifty-nine they will call me and say they need
> more time. We'll go back and forth, and blah, blah,
> money, blah, blah. I talk, they talk. Eventually,
> something happens, and maybe someone publishes
> your next book, and all this takes at least a year.
> Does this make sense to you?*

I answered:

> *It took a while, but I found a translator. He
> recommends I email you less.*

Legally Tender Validation

One day after providing yet another ungrateful client with
my consulting services, I plodded out to the mailbox, and
there—among the stacks of bills, the forty-seven Bed Bath
& Beyond twenty-percent-off coupons, the twice-weekly
requests from the NRA for money, and a collection notice
regarding the John Wayne movie library I'd ordered from
Columbia House—lay an inconspicuous-looking envelope
with my publisher's return address on it. Fearing it might
be a slander lawsuit launched by the hapless book cover
designer, I ripped it open with heavy heart.

My advance.

Don't get too excited for me.

It was small. So small, in fact, that the actual number will remain cloaked in mystery. So low that aspiring writers don't *want* to know the number. And so low that, well, getting paid only fifteen percent of that teeny-tiny number was a pretty good reason for my agent to treat me the way he did.

But, hey. Screw that! I got paid! There was no turning back. My publisher *really was* going to print my book and ship the copies to bookstores, and the above-one-hundred-IQ crowd would be able to judge my writing without any further interference. And if I made ten percent on every book sold, and we sold, say, four or five million copies at $24.95, then … then … then that's not bad, right? Sure, most rookie authors are lucky to sell a couple of thousand books at most, and all the money they end up with in the end is the advance—but that wouldn't be me! I'd, like, defy all the odds, pay back my advance, and bank at least enough money to … to drink craft beer for a week?

ENOUGH ABOUT YOU. LET'S TALK ABOUT ME.

BecoolBecoolBecool

Finally, finally, finally, another piece of the publishing glacier broke free and washed my quest for fame and fortune a tiny bit forward: Allison, the publishing company's publicist, called. Not the "director of communications" or the "PR director," but the *publicist*. As in, it is her profession to blatantly seek publicity for me and my book. Why did this titillate me so? Because back in the ad agency world, we danced around the word *publicity* as if it were obscene.

Of course, my clients *wanted* publicity—regular, old, cut-it-out-for-the-scrapbook, hey-I-saw-you-in-the-paper publicity—but we buffered them from the "crudeness" of actually stating this desire by sitting in meetings and discussing strategy, positioning, and editorial calendars.

And now, the shoe was on the other foot. Now I'd become Narcissus, seeking my own reflection in the pool. Kindly, however, Allison spared me the embarrassment of double-talking my way around the need for publicity by introducing herself as "a *publicist*." Sweet.

After she identified herself, her first few sentences blew past my ears for no other reason than the volume of my self-lecture: *Dude! Be cool! She can either do a lot for you, or very little. So be cool. Be cool. Be cool. Sound appreciative. Sound informed. Sound excited, but not giddy. Sound like a professional. Be cool.*

After managing to clue back in, I figured out she was talking about my book tour.

"Initially," she said, "we want to commit to Miami, Palm Springs, Raleigh-Durham, Atlanta, and a good bit of South Carolina."

My mind once again stepped out for a quick fantasy as the most important conversation of my life faded off into Charlie-Brown-Teacher speak. I was *gone*, baby. My brain wasn't within a twelve-hour drive of that conversation: Location, Miami—no, South Beach—gliding onto the patio of a bookstore bar (in slow motion) for a signing event, as anorexic models with boob jobs swooned all around me. I gleefully ignored Al Franken, who stood grumpily about thirtieth in line. Carl Hiaasen and Tim Dorsey bullied their way to my side and wished me well.

I generously offered little air kisses to ex-girlfriends, and nodded with Clintonesque understanding as they threatened to slash their wrists and begged for one more chance.

"So, I'll email you this document, and you use it as a reference," Allison said, employing that universal *gotta-go, end-of-the-conversation* lilt. "Do you have any questions?"

"No, this is great," I said. "Just great. Really great. This is great."

"Well, uh, great," she said. "Email me the document when you're done, and be sure to let me know anyone you want galley proofs sent to."

"Galley proofs?"

"Yes—those are the uncorrected proofs we make from an early version of the manuscript. Just cheap paperbacks. It's what larger publishers send out to reviewers and other VIPs we want to see the book in advance."

"When do these galley proofs arrive?"

"We have them already," Allison said.

"Will you send me one? I'd like to try and sell it on eBay."

Okay, I didn't say that. Didn't even think that. In reality, those words didn't come to me until a couple weeks later, but—well, as a writer, I'm granting myself the creative license to "exist in the eternal present," so I can move stuff around if the need arises. The real end of the conversation went more like this:

"Any questions?"

"No, but thanks—this is great!"

"You've only got ninety days before bookstores start sending copies of your book back. So you'll need to hustle. Cool?"

"Cool."

"No questions?"

"No questions."

"Okay. Buh-bye."

Click. Dial tone.

So not cool. So not, not cool. Ninety days, *and you said you had no questions?*

How about, "Is gas money provided for a book tour? Air transportation? Coach or business class? Food per diem? Lodging? Ritz, Holiday Inn, or Motel Six? When will these tour dates be? Why did you pick those cities? Can we add more cities? When is the book coming out? Will you send me some of those galley proofs? When do the actual books arrive? When a friend hosts a function for me, are books sold on behalf of the publisher? Or am I selling books I buy myself at the author's discount? Are you doing any marketing? Where are you sending books? Who is doing the follow-up on the books you send out? And who, dammit, who among us doesn't love NASCAR?"

I stood and looked at the phone with self-loathing. A week later, Allison miraculously sent me an unsolicited email answering my questions. A good sign, no? Make room at the top, bitches—there's gonna be a new bestselling sheriff in town!

Doing My Homework

For the next couple of days, I waded through my homework for Allison, which essentially entailed building a database of affinity groups that might be predisposed to buy my book, then tracking down the appropriate point of contact for each group's magazine or newsletter. In my case, those groups included the Marines, Auburn University, Kappa Alpha Order (my college frat), my high school Porter Gaud, and all my contacts within the South Carolina media. Just to make sure all the bases were covered, I also jotted down the names of several bartenders I tipped a lot, a couple of cops who'd put me in handcuffs for "misunderstandings," and this one dancer I knew who was "working her way through college." Doing this work was almost as boring as reading about it—thus, the quick demise of this particular section.

Pondering the Deadly Sins?

Every day, we read about celebrities imploding. They seem to have it all, then go full–Matthew Perry, time after time. Drugs, alcoholism, car crashes, arrests, overdoses, out-of-wedlock kids, tantrums, tirades, nervous breakdowns, depression—their bios read like the notes from a Kardashian family Christmas dinner.

At the risk of sounding French, I do confess to a petite nugget of empathy for their madness. This empathy doesn't surface as a result of any great wisdom, but instead from morbid fascination and some deep thinking (by my standards) about the world where *they* live. Consider their lives: All gravitational norms that ground us as humans have ceased to exist in their world, so the darker side of their human nature is free to go transition from Hannah Montana to Miley Cyrus. After all, who needs God when you *are* a god? Imagine a life where you could simply banish anyone who makes you in the least bit unhappy. No, forget that: You could banish anyone who dared even look you in the eyes with disapproval. Sounds savory, no?

But here's the rub: Before you even realized the negative effects of all this banishing, a new inner circle of yes-men would step in to "help" you. Bowing and scraping, they'd gently lift those heavy reins of banishment from you and assume for themselves the task of monitoring your posse, ensuring that only their circle of remora fish will be allowed to feed on your scraps.

Why? Self-preservation, of course. If *they* can fashion a world where you are right/smart/perfect/funny 24/7/365, then it stands to reason that *you* will be happy in this new world. You following me? And if *you* find yourself happy, then *you* are going to try to maintain the status quo—a status quo that includes *them* inside your inner circle. In medical terms, you've contracted a deadly virus, but you love the feeling the virus causes.

Next stop, Perfectville, inhabited only by folks who think *you* are the Sun King, no matter what you do. And since you haven't *personally* banished anyone in quite some time, this would feel strangely natural, this Perfectville. You haven't hand-chosen these people who surround you; ergo, the world revolves around you because … the world revolves around you. Every joke you tell is funny, every insight you have is brilliant, and every cause you back is righteous.

Wake up at two P.M. from a horrific three-day bender, drag yourself to the bathroom to die, and—ta-da! There's a living room full of "friends" telling you how awesome and funny and cool you've been … for three straight days. The best! Everyone loves you! Want a Grey Goose Bloody Mary (that you paid for)? How about a Valium? *It's right here*, sayeth the parasites of Perfectville.

Now, let's consider the unthinkable: What would happen if a couple of Joes like you and me got an invitation to move into our very own Perfectville? To snuggle up with the seven deadly sins on a daily basis? Would we take it? What about if the invitation came with you already understanding the pitfalls described above? Would you be willing to forfeit your spot as a face in the crowd? Take the risk that you could supervise the sycophants and rebuff the bootlickers?

Now, consider the phone call that came in one day:

ALLISON: Prioleau? It's me, Allison. Uh, you're not going to believe this, but I just got a call from a producer at *Oprah*. They want to know if you have any photos of yourself working these minimum-wage jobs.

(Insert sound of crickets)

ALLISON: Hello?

(More crickets)

ALLISON: Prioleau?

ME: Oprah? As in talk show *Oprah*?

ALLISON: That's her.

ME: Billionaire Oprah?

ALLISON: You got it.

ME: Well, uh, I took some snapshots—but nothing fancy.

ALLISON: That's okay. This is just an inquiry, so there's no way to know if it will pan out.

ME: Probably for the best if it doesn't work out. My book makes *A Million Little Pieces* look like a deposition given by an Amish elder on sodium pentothal.

(Insert more crickets)

ME: Ha! That's a joke! Aren't I funny?

So, Oprah. The undisputed heavyweight bookseller, Oprah. The spiritual advisor to more Americans than the Pope-ah, Oprah. How big is Oprah in the literary world? If *The New York Times Book Review* printed an entire *weekend edition* exploring the brilliance of your book, sales would be gentle summer rain compared to being smacked by Hurricane Oprah.

Now, how on Earth does some yo-yo-yokel from Charleston, South Carolina, contend with an invitation to appear on Oprah? If such an invite transpired, many issues would demand consideration ... but first things first: I'd need to decide which *me* Oprah would meet.

The Christian Me, where I act all humble and kind?

Maybe the Bookselling Me, where I lie about how I wrote the book as a selfless attempt to shed light on the plight of the less fortunate?

Or the Actual Me, where I grovel and weep and beg her viewers to buy my book because I can't bear one more day as a marketing consultant, and my wife will leave me if I go back to spending my days watching funny videos on YouTube? Which "you" would *you* use? Which one would go over the best in Oprahoma? I decided there was only one person mean enough to set me straight: my agent.

ME: Dude, Allison called. She got an inquiry from a producer at *Oprah*.

AGENT: %&$y ... Don't $!+, M^* joke with me ... {+%$*"!!!

ME: I'm *not* joking. She just called, and they asked for some photos of me sweatin' for the big bucks.

AGENT: Sweet! Well done!

ME: Do you think I'll get sued by one of my subjects if I go on *Oprah*, and the book makes it big?

AGENT: I think you're gonna get sued by *all* of your subjects, whether you go on *Oprah* or not.

ME: If I get sued, will you accept fifteen percent of the liability? Hello? Hello?

I Can Feel My Head Swelling Already

It had been a week since the *Oprah* producer called Allison, which begat my day of running around getting photos scanned and emailed off to Oprah. Here's how many phone calls and emails I'd gotten from or about Oprah that week: zero. Here's how many people I'd killed as a result: zero. Here's how many I was going to kill if I didn't hear something soon: a lot.

Two Weeks Post-Oprah, No Word …

All work and no play makes Jack a dull boy. All work and no play makes Jack a dull boy. All work and no play makes Jack a dull boy. All work and no play makes Jack a dull boy.

All work and no play makes Jack a dull boy. All work and no play makes Jack a dull boy. All work and no play makes Jack a dull boy. All work and no play makes Jack a dull boy.

All work and no play makes Jack a dull boy. All work and no play makes Jack a dull boy. All work and no play makes Jack a dull boy. All work and no play makes Jack a dull boy.

All work and no play makes Jack a dull boy. All work and no play makes Jack a dull boy. All work and no play makes Jack a dull boy. All work and no play makes Jack a dull boy.

Meh, Probably for the Best

The more I thought about it, I'm not sure I was cut out to be an *Oprah* guest anyway. I'd probably end up like most of her author-guests: Blast off to the moon … make some decent money … become sort of a dick … fail to sell my next book … come crashing down to Earth … then try and de-dick-ify my reputation among all my friends who saw me acting like a dick.

We'll never know.

MORE ME, ME, ME

One day, Allison called. And we talked about me. Me, and my book tour. I rarely talk about me, and people who talk about me are usually pointing out that I owe them money, so "me" being spoken of in a positive way was exciting. Upon hanging up, I decided the time had arrived to take a look at the man in the mirror, and perhaps wrestle with the Hollywood starlet who was trying to sleep her way up the ladder to the forefront of my consciousness.

Why? Because the topic of "me" was getting just a tad too much facetime at the podium. I was beginning to think like one of those clients who'd burned me out back in the ad biz, believing my needs and position somehow *entitled* me to a greater share of Allison's attention. This is a difficult thing to process for a guy who thinks the words *me* and *entitled* go together like *Whoopi* and *thong*.

The conversation mostly entailed me listening and Allison explaining what she was up to. Arranging a book tour for a first-time author is no easy task, because it means asking bookstore owners who've carefully built a following of readers/buyers to throw caution to the wind and host an event for an author who could arrive and go over like a Gordon Ramsay review of a Hot Pocket.

The book tour is the big thing, right? The here-I-am symbol of making it as a writer? What could happen out there? Who might I meet? How many people will cram themselves into the room for the opportunity to see me looking over my reading glasses, uttering pithy and life-changing wisdom nuggets? All that was needed was for Allison to set up the dates, and I'd be SpaceXed to Mars.

Her current focus, Allison explained, was on organizing my jaunt around the southeast. I'm happy to report that I did not miss any of this conversation due to errant fantasies, nor did I press her to do more, nor did I ask her if she'd heard from Oprah. In fact, I managed to repeat my previous performance on the phone, which revolved around me saying "That's great" and failing to ask a single pertinent question.

Note to self: Get Allison to call after 5:30 P.M. when you've got a couple of bracers onboard. It certainly couldn't hurt.

The Sun Also Sets

One day, as part of this great adventure, I met the poet laureate of South Carolina. Did you even know that South Carolina *has* a poet laureate? Me, neither. But it's nice to know we have a fancy book-learnin' position like that down here in the Palmetto State. The only poems I know start with the lines "*There once was a man from Nantucket,*" and "*They scrub these walls to stop my pen,*" so it's delightful to discover we have at least one person in the state qualified to laureate. Because South Carolina is always forty-ninth in every category (thank God for Mississippi), the question came to mind when I met her: "Are you the forty-ninth-best state poet laureate?" Happily, however, discretion won the battle for my tongue. If ever appointed "humorist laureate," I would consider that question punch-worthy, so my piehole remained shut. Still, I wondered about Mississippi, and if they had themselves good enough couth to have an official Rhymin' Writer.

Anyway, my awareness of this young lady laureate came from my novelist friend Beth. We'd spoken briefly on the phone a few days earlier, then I lucked into encountering the poet laureate with Beth at a library literary event. She's the sweet, upbeat, wild-eyed type that one hopes for when meeting a poet.

"So you're Prioleau!" she said.

"And you are the highest ranking poet I've ever met."

"I looked up your publisher on the web, and I love them! Incredible literary integrity, real diversity—too cool! You should be very proud they picked you up!"

"Well, thanks. I'm just a rookie, but my agent thinks the world of them."

"When do you ship?"

(Note: Apparently, I ship. Cool.)

"The official publishing date is in six weeks."

"Too cool! How are the reviews?"

"Uh, no reviews, yet."

"Really?"

"Yeah. No reviews, yet."

"Huh. Well, are you all set for your book tour?"

"It's coming up. Nothing firm yet."

"And your publishing date is when?"

"Six weeks. I gotta tell you, Marjory—you're makin' me a little nervous here."

"Nah, don't worry."

Across the room was an event organizer in khaki directing people to their seats. He raised his microphone. Marjory moved to her seat, pressing her hands into mine.

"It'll work out," she said. "I'm sure it will all come together."

"Yes," I said. "Isn't it pretty to think so?"

I then went for a walk. In the rain. To die.

Shiny, Happy People

Over the next couple of weeks, my pal Allison began chipping away at the task of book-tour building. Within a few weeks, it looked fairly respectable, and I started turning down invitations to social events because "I'd love to but, damn, I'm on my *book tour*." It didn't matter if the event actually fell on the same date as a speaking engagement—I just felt like a bigshot saying it. During the tour-building process, one of the bookstore owners Allison pitched on hosting an event responded with a delightfully hilarious email.

The bookstore owner's remarks are in italics, and my thoughts regarding her smarmy remarks are in bold.

I can't believe this writer thought it would be better to hold multiple jobs where you're hardly paid enough to live, much less save any money. His premise shows how ignorant some people are in corporate America.

Did I just read that? Time to parry, methinks! This email is going to bring to light how some people in America are so pissed at the world that they don't recognize humor when it hits them upside their wrinkled, bitter visage.

What about "generation debt"? Individuals with degrees who can't find work that allows them to survive?

I haven't heard of that, but I *have* heard of dumb-ass debt. It's the never-ending tale of a hundred thousand dumb-asses a year who attend college on student loans, don't work while they're in school, go on spring break with the rich kids as if it's their right, then graduate with a completely useless degree in things like Eskimo history or filmmaking. Hint: Unless you're very lucky, college is four years of work, not fun ... and the point of that work is to study in a field that will yield ... well, work. Do you know a lot of unemployed engineers, pharmacists, or computer-science majors? Yes, it's painful that the women's studies industry isn't hiring at the moment, but the U.S. military is always looking for folks with a bachelor's degree.

Consider the tens of thousands of people who aren't even able to get a college degree and HAVE to work those simple jobs that he takes because they are caught in an unequal and unfair system.

Stop! Really? The system works *against* the little guy? Damn, I need to learn more about these minimum-wage multitudes. A lot more. Maybe I'll ... I'll ... I know! I'll take a year and go work minimum-wage jobs! Note to self: Keep a diary or something.

Is this even a realistic account of their lives?

Excellent question. But how could one uncover the answer? There must be *some* trick for unearthing the ideas buried between the front and back covers of a book. There must be *some* way to find out what it says! Think, Prioleau, think! She's crying out for help! Must … crack … code!

If he was a white-collar big shot, he probably has money that could carry him through his old age.

That's it! *That's* the secret! You glance at the title, ignore the book jacket, overlook the review comments by insignificant writers like Pat Conroy, then project your very own wild conjecture onto all those pages.

I haven't read the book, of course, so I'm willing to read what he has to say.

Yes, certainly you are. Humorless, virtue-signaling types are often known for their open-mindedness, always willing to discuss ideas they find e motionally problematic in a calm, cool, reasonable, logic-and-reason-driven manner. Let's get together for a chat over fava-bean salad and a nice Chianti.

This is my initial reaction to the book, though, and I don't want our customers to have a similar experience during a signing at our store.

This is your *initial* reaction??!! My God, then why go further? Your emotions have spoken, and what you *feel* is the way things are!

This is not a humorous issue, and if this book is making fun of the situation, I'm not interested.

In fact, I'm going to hold my breath until everyone agrees with the things I feel.

If you think there are things I need to know, by all means, let me know!

That way, I can feel superior to you by passive-aggressively getting you to invest more of your time on my behalf, then feel superior (times infinity) by refusing to accept your added commentary.

Thanks for contacting us.

In the future, however, please know I am only interested in books on (or by) people who are dysfunctional, persecuted, defeated, disabled, depressed, or diseased. When I read, I like to feel good about myself by feeling emotional on their behalf.

Why have I taken the time to include this? Because no matter what you write or the genre you choose, there are going to be people who will attack you—viciously. Forewarned is forearmed.

REALLY? REAL ESTATE?

Facing the Wall

One day, a friend mentioned to me, "Hey, Prioleau—I saw your poster at Barnes and Noble for your signing. Too cool!"

Oddly, he didn't follow up with one of the usual backhanded comments so many folks feel required to use: "Wow—you're a real live, famous author now," or "You'll remember us when you're big and famous, right?" I don't know why people feel compelled to make these sorts of remarks. After all, no one reads about a banker friend in the paper and says, "Ohh! Big Loan Guy ... remember us regular checking-account folks when you start hanging with Warren Buffett." But someone who gets a break in music, acting, writing? The semi-insulting response is hardwired into us, like our need to tell a bereaved friend, "It's part of God's plan," as if God's primary job is to serve as some sort of Celestial Assassin.

Anyway, this buddy made mention of the poster, and I figured the local Barnes and Noble had finally put out my book. Probably not a bad idea, since I'm within two degrees of separation from every book-buying soul who resides in the town of Mount Pleasant. And I live five miles away. And my signing event was fast approaching. I didn't really think too much about it for a couple of days, but then an errand steered me right by the store, and curiosity got the best of me. The next thing I knew, the car parked itself.

So this was it. The moment when, after fourteen years of banging away on a keyboard in an obsessive quest for publication, my first book would emerge within a real bookstore context. My ugly mug would be there on a poster, with actual sales-oriented copy announcing, "HE WROTE SOMETHING THAT DIDN'T SUCK." There would be real shelf space, trumpeting the fact that my non-sucky book had managed to slip past all the built-in defenses: agents, publishers, editors, sales reps, and store buyers, all with a sworn duty to defend the public from suckage in print. This was it.

Approaching the entrance, I simply could not help but wonder where the poster would be, where the books would be, and if, as a local-boy-done-good, there might be a table set aside for *my* book.

Alone now. High noon. Only a glass door separated me from an intoxicating blast of endorphins. I pushed it open ... and there, staring right back at me, front and frickin' center ... was the picture of some mega-smile lady who writes beach-based romance novels, who had a signing in two weeks.

No problem! So the poster wasn't in the entrance foyer. It was probably next to my table display.

Let's see. Ah! The "New Arrivals" table—it was probably there. I did a 360-degree inspection. Nuthin'. Another 360 degrees. Nuthin'.

Oh! Of course! There was the new nonfiction table: 360. 360 again. Nuthin'.

The "Staff Recommends" table: Nuthin'.

Humor section: scan left, scan right, left, right, check alphabetically. Nuthin'.

Local authors section: scan, scan, scan, scan, alphabet. Nuthin'.

Memoirs table: 270-degree scan—Christ, that's Hillary; please not here, not with her—remaining 90 degrees. Nuthin'.

Store scan: up, down, back, forth, forth, down, up, back. Nuthin'.

Store re-scan: zig, zag, knick, knack, paddy whack. And so on.

High noon, plus fifteen. Leaving. Passing through the foyer where the beach-romance scrivener's poster had stolen my thunder. Wait! I realized her poster had a *reverse* side, facing the wall. Could it be? Could the reverse side be my … and there it was. And so it goes. Such is the nature of things.

Before ending this section, and having discovered the ugly truth about most big-box booksellers, I'll let you in on a secret: These places aren't in the book business—they're in the real-estate business, which is sold by the inch. If a publisher wants three books on the shelf, they have to pay up. If they want a book facing out, showing the cover instead of the spine, pay up. If they want it on one of these featured tables, pay up. You could write a book arguing about the mathematics of string theory, and if you send in the check, it'll be right there on the "Hot New Fiction" table.

Wanna know why you've got to work on marketing your book if a smaller publishing house chooses to publish your stuff? You just read the reason.

Almost six hundred Barnes and Noble locations exist here in the land of the free … and huge publishers enjoy huge discounts, because they rent space in volume. They have people whose only job is to negotiate the rental rate, and they check up on the placement they paid for. They have people whose only job is to keep track of the space they rented, how long the rental lasts, and whether the rental spaces are producing the expected sales. We're talking spreadsheets, and analytics, and nerdy people calculating ROI.

It doesn't matter if the book is good or not; what matters is that they spent the money to print it. And because they printed it, they need it to sell.

Do you think a boutique publishing house maintains this level of resources? No—they're too busy trying to explain to you and me what a comma splice is. They're arguing with you and me about the use of recycled paper. They're dealing with a passive-aggressive graphic designer who thinks their design is "ruined" because the book title needs to be one font size larger.

The good news, however, is that the odds are solid your small publisher won't mind at all if you undertake nine trips to the Barnes and Noble headquarters trying to find who's in charge of space rentals, then negotiate a rate, then find the next space available is January of next year.

DIY marketing is likely your best option.

My First Book Signing

The evening of my first book signing finally arrived. I spent a week individually emailing every single person in my address book, by name, telling them the book was available through online booksellers, and—if they were from Charleston—the dates and places of my two signings. The feedback was amazing. If a mere one in three people who said they would be there showed up, the Mount Pleasant riot police would no doubt get the chance to use some of their crowd-control toys.

"I really think I should warn the store," I told my wife. "There might be three hundred people there. It will be embarrassing if there aren't enough books for everyone."

My wife, the one in the family with a triple-digit IQ, assuaged my concerns.

"Let's just hope for a hundred," she said. "That would be huge."

I kept my mouth shut, but I was pretty sure she was wrong.

I got to the Barnes and Noble about thirty minutes early, where I was met by a knockout named Emily. It immediately dawned on me that I should have included pictures of my wife and Emily in my email. ("Come see Emily and Heidi standing next to each other for only $24.95, and get a free book!")

"This is my first time," I told Emily. "I have no idea what I'm doing, so be gentle."

"It's pretty complex," she explained. "You sit here, and when someone walks up, you sign their book."

Mention crowd control, I told myself. Let Emily know. You owe it to her. She's being very sweet, and she has no idea that in thirty minutes, men with shields and sticks are going to be beating her customers. Maybe her, too. And when they fire the tear-gas grenades, someone is going to get hurt. Speak up! Say something!

"Uh, Emily?"

"Yes?"

"I, uh, there's something you need to be aware of ... "

"Yes?"

Her professional career was in my hands. But my wife's words lingered in my mind.

"I ... I ... don't have a pen."

"I think I can solve that issue."

And then, pen in hand, I waited. I checked right and left for a place to seek cover, eyes scanning for a spot that could contain both me and my bride when the rioting began. Locating a floor vent would be primo, enabling us to gulp fresh air as the tear gas rained down. I felt conflicted: I had failed to protect my kin and kind, but all I could do now was wait. And sweat.

Tick-tock, tick-tock.

7:10 P.M.

Once upon an evening dreary, while I sat there alone
and weary,
Amongst many volumes of self-help lore,
While I nodded, nearly napping, suddenly there came a tapping,
As of someone gently rapping, rapping at the bookstore door.
'Tis my wife, I muttered, tapping at that big glass door—
Only this, and nothing more.

I heard again and my eyes unshuttered, when, with many a
flirt and flutter,

In there stepped a stately stranger, dressed in tweed like days
   of yore.
But, with mien of English professor, came straight through
   the bookstore door,
And strode straight to me, shoes 'a-clicking on the floor,
But he browsed, and nothing more.

"Professor!" said I, "you bring me evil! — whether you're
   teacher or the devil!
By that Heaven that bends above us—by that God we
   both adore—
Tell this soul that's totally bumming, if anyone is
   actually coming,
Humiliation cloaks my body, is that what I am here for?
Will I sell at this bookstore? When will a buyer walk through
   the door?"
Quoth the tweed man, "Nevermore."

7:30 P.M., and the Lord Has Taken Mercy

The crowd drifted in, and the store got crowded. During the next two hours, about two hundred friends and family came through the store. You've been in crowded stores before, so I won't spend a lot of time enchanting you with nouns and adjectives that don't move the story along. Instead, what I will tell you is how it felt:

1. Humbling—Anyone willing to get in their car on a rainy Thursday night to come to something as inherently boring as a book-signing event is a real friend. It is a time when you get to see, firsthand, the people on whom you've had a positive effect—because no one there had anything to gain by showing up. I'm a nobody, and I have no way to reciprocate, other than with friendship. If I'd gotten this book published when I was in the advertising business, the joint would have been awash in vendors and salespeople, each doing their job. But now? These kind souls were taking time out of their very busy schedules to cheer me on, and the feeling was nothing less than humbling.

2. Goofy—Of the hundred books I sold that night, a total of six went to people I didn't know. (Keep that in mind—the importance of marketing, and reaching out to people you know. I'm told selling a hundred books is a huge deal, but it only happened because I connected with every person I knew within twenty miles.) Although my bride would berate me for saying so, I felt goofy. If I stood on the side of the road with a sign that said, "Why lie? I want a beer," every one of those friends who saw me would have pulled over and given me a twenty and a lift to the bar. They attended that Thursday night as friends, and the actual words on the pages of my book ranked about twentieth in

their reasons to attend. So I felt goofy. But I also felt magnificent that my wife and I had touched that many people's lives. The experience put into perspective the elusive pursuit of happiness.

DANCING WITH MYSELF

The Wacky World of Work Ethic

As mentioned, my current life revolves around consulting and striving to be a full-time, financially successful author. Consulting is a weird gig, because just about the time you feel like another job will never surface, it does—and the pay-scale for a no-overhead consultant is just sick enough to soothe the savage money beast that thrashes about within every checkbook. It's fairly difficult to justify to yourself getting even a white-collar job when simply resisting that urge results in the same-sized paycheck that used to come at the end of a month for a *week's* work.

Truth be known, it's not a very hard job, either. A client calls and says, "I need problem X solved." You say, "Give me a week, and let's meet." You meet, and you say, "Based on my twenty years of experience, you need to do Y." The client says, "Hmm. Not Z? I went to a seminar once and they said Z would solve X." You say, "Z is certainly a possibility." The client says, "You think?" You say, "Absolutely. Not what I would do, but what do I know?" The client says, "Thank you." You send the client a bill.

However, there's a weird part to leaving the forty-hour work week—because, after almost twenty years in the professional world, having plenty of time to do something you love doesn't come easy. There is a tiny nagging voice in the back of your mind that haunts you every day, bitching about the fact that you aren't playing by the normal societal rules. Here's my latest internal conversation:

VOICE: So, what do you have on tap today?

ME: Well, you little bastard, I'm going to go to the bank and deposit this big, fat check I got for writing and producing that corporate video.

VOICE: Well, good for you. Is it enough to live on?

ME: For a bit.

VOICE: That's really good. How about home insurance? You got that covered? Car insurance? Life insurance? Flood insurance? Personal articles insurance? Catastrophic health insurance?

ME: Can't I just enjoy *today*, you little son of a bitch?

VOICE: Of course! All you need is three meals, a cot, and a roof over your head, right?

ME: That's what I think. Well, that's what the new me thinks.

VOICE: I agree. So, does the new you have groceries covered? And money for property taxes, car repairs, home repairs, water bill, electric bill, phone bill, internet connection, cell phone bill, and pest control?

ME: Eat me. I've got my health.

VOICE: Yes. Yes, you do. But do you have the money for the prescriptions that keep you healthy? Cash to put in the HSA savings account? Some extra dough for vet bills? Those pups need their health, too.

ME: I will not be dictated to by you, you pessimistic little paraquat.

VOICE: Yes, but you will be dictated to by Caesar, right? And render unto him what is his? So, thirty percent of that check will be set aside for taxes, right?

ME: Look—I'm trying to break free of all that crap. I don't want to be constrained by the norms of society.

VOICE: Guess you should've thought about that before you followed the societal norms right down the aisle to the responsibilities of marriage.

ME: Religious norms.

VOICE: Whatever. Society … religion … peer pressure. All the same to me—gives us something to banter about.

ME: What the hell do you want from me?

VOICE: Toil, you lazy, worthless, unproductive sloth. Unhappy, dark-to-dark, full-body-sweat, stress-filled toil. Everyone else in the world is toiling, but you— you put shaving on your list of things to do! Get back to work.

ME: And if I refuse?

VOICE: Then I'll be here to whisper sweet poetry into your ear. All day.

ME: Can I ask you to *please* leave me alone?

VOICE: Be happy to … as soon as you tell me where *you* end and *I* start.

ME: You know, I could just have a few beers and drown you out.

VOICE: It's nine A.M.

ME: I mean later, at Happy Hour.

VOICE: Feel free. You have fun. Stay up late. Party hearty. I'll be sure to wake you up early so we can get an early start tomorrow.

And so it goes.

There is good news, though. There are four ways I can shut the voice up: beer, obviously; consulting work; writing; and promoting myself as an author or a consultant.

And there's more good news. There's an unlimited amount of promoting to be done, because a publisher— large or small—can't afford to invest much in a first-time author. In musical terms, it just doesn't make much sense to sign Corporal Tunnel and the Syndromes and book Wrigley Field as their first gig. If the good Corporal and the boys want to make it big, they need to get out there and get noticed. When records start selling, the label gets busy capitalizing on the momentum. But as a guy who spent fourteen years sweating the tiniest details of my clients' advertising, marketing, and public relations, I realized somebody needed to start getting jiggy on my behalf.

So, where does one begin to promote a new author? I'm a marketing guy, I told myself—I've done this stuff before. I've done this a thousand times before. I'll just interview myself with the same questions I used to interview new clients and take it from there:

MARKETING ME: Okay, first—what's the marketing budget?

WRITER ME: Zero.

MARKETING ME: The budget can't be zero. Now, how much is it?

WRITER ME: You tell me.

MARKETING ME: You sound like all the yo-yos I used to work for.

WRITER ME: Well, maybe I'm trying to elicit a little empathy here.

MARKETING ME: Okay. Forget it. Who's the target market?

WRITER ME: Every adult in America.

MARKETING ME: Tighter, please.

WRITER ME: Every book-buying adult in America.

MARKETING ME: Try again.

WRITER ME: Book-buying adults, college educated.

MARKETING ME: Okay, we're down to about twenty-five million here. How else can we tighten it up?

WRITER ME: They need to get my sense of humor.

MARKETING ME: That takes us from twenty-five million down to you, your wife, and fourteen of your closest friends. Let's go a little wider.

WRITER ME: They need a sense of humor?

MARKETING ME: I can't work with someone as dumb as you.

WRITER ME: Great. Now I've got the Voice nagging me and you firing me.

MARKETING ME: Well, throw me a frickin' bone. Give me something. How do *you* decide what books you are going to read?

WRITER ME: Someone tells me about them.

MARKETING ME: Okay, so we need word-of-mouth buzz. How do the people who tell you get told about these books in the first place?

WRITER ME: Someone tells them?

MARKETING ME: Magically? Like how life magically began in Darwin's theory?

WRITER ME: Hmm, maybe not.

MARKETING ME: Here's the plan: I'm going to go work for someone who has a budget. You, uh, start emailing. Email every single person in your address book, and personalize every single message. They need to know you wrote them specifically.

WRITER ME: Got it.

MARKETING ME: If they write back, you respond. Personally. And no "Thanks!" crap. You write them back, thank them for responding, ask them how the kids are, and beg them to email and call their friends. I don't care if they write back ten times; you respond in depth every single time.

WRITER ME: That sounds like a lot of work.

MARKETING ME: You either invest money or you invest time. You've got no money, but plenty of time. Unless, of course, this will interfere with your nap routine.

WRITER ME: Does it matter that I became a writer so I could be a writer, not a self-promoting organ grinder?

MARKETING ME: You can always write muffler-shop radio ads.

WRITER ME: One email campaign, comin' up!

Let me tell you: Writing an individual email to every single person in your address book is no small task. Even if you copy and paste the meat-and-potatoes portion, it takes *days*. And, if you look through your email address book, you'll find dozens and dozens of folks who are acquaintance-type friends you haven't corresponded with since you were using AOL on dial-up. If you write them an email about your having published a book, the one thing they *aren't* going to think is, "Awesome! My kind-of-a-friend Prioleau got a book published! I'll bet he's really busy, so I better not bother him. I'll just quietly and effectively notify everyone I know who might be interested." No, ma'am. They want to know the details. And how you've been. And when you can get together.

It's exhausting, but it pays off.

Let me explain something about this marketing gig, by addressing the question, "How do you know if it works? Does it sell books?"

Boutique publisher? You know it works, because your publisher will call you and say, "Hey, keep up the good work! We're getting orders!"

Big publisher? You'll have no clue. ... The books belong to the corporate giant, and your efforts result in sales unbeknownst to you. In the case of my first book, no one at the publisher ever reported sales to me. I just knew that no one cared about my book more than I did, and if I hoped to achieve the vaunted word-of-mouth, it would be my efforts that made it happen.

Remember, however, what I said back at the beginning: The item you're selling ain't a painting that's consumable in a glance. Or a four-minute song that takes, well, four minutes to experience. You ain't inviting someone to attend a play you're in, which might result in a surprisingly good time. It's a big, fat, no-promises book.

With that said, allow me to tell you about my mistakes in personally marketing *You Want Fries With That?*

To sell anything, you need an elevator pitch, right? A quick summation of the benefits the product offers, and why you, the potential customer, will probably commit suicide if you don't have it.

You Want Fries With That? came into being for one primary purpose: to make readers laugh. And (I'm being uncomfortably braggadocious here) it did. In fact, it might be the funniest nonfiction book ever written, assuming you exclude the ingenious ponderings of P. J. O'Rourke. I've had no less than a dozen readers confess they read it on an airplane, and were laughing so hard the passengers around them interrupted to ask what the book was.

My sales pitch? "It's about a year when I worked minimum-wage jobs—if it doesn't make you laugh your ass off, I'll buy it back."

That elevator pitch sucked, because "humor" is risky. There's no guarantee to the potential customer that your writing is, in fact, funny. Now you're asking them to trust you, and when it comes to writing, believe me … no one does.

What I should have said is, "I took a year and worked minimum-wage jobs to see what the experience would be like through the eyes of someone with twenty years of business experience, see for myself the level of insanity these poor souls went through, meet some of them, and tell their story. Oh, and I'll bet you the cost of the book it will also make you laugh your ass off."

With this pitch, I've given them a reason to buy the book, and the subjective humor is a bonus.

What will your elevator pitch be for your crime-fiction novel? Hell, I don't know—but you'd be wise to talk about why you wrote the book, why you developed the characters you did, and what insights the reader will gain—beyond just reading an exciting, fun, and well-written book.

The Big Day Arriveth

My book was finally out into the world—not just to the local Barnes and Noble, but the whole wide world! The noise generated by the public the day I hit the market made a sensory deprivation tank sound like a Who concert. I began to grow concerned. Little did I know the worst was yet to come.

OKAY. I ADMIT IT. THE MONEY MATTERS.

Isn't There a Part of This Where I *Make* Money?

I'm no public relations expert, but—wait. Actually, I *am* a public relations expert. In fact, people used to pay my firm two hundred fifty dollars an hour for me to advise them on public relations. So let me give a very brief primer on the way the "media relations" part of public relations works:

1. You, the client, tell me you want some issue covered by some particular media outlet. Perhaps several media outlets.

2. I dispatch to the appropriate reporter an in-depth package on the topic, which covers in advance all the stuff that might force the journalist to have to do actual work. In short, the package includes

the "who, what, when, where, and why" that is important to the journalist's readers.

3. I follow up with the journalist via telephone.
4. I follow up with the journalist via email.
5. I follow up with the journalist via handwritten note on stationery.
6. I repeat Steps 3, 4, and 5 over and over and over and over and over until the journalist covers the story simply to avoid the hassle of filing a restraining order against me.

Based on my experience in the business, Step 1 without Steps 2, 3, 4, 5, and 6 would be as useless as trying to achieve peace in the Middle East by blaming the problems on the one country in the region that owns nukes but no oil. To get *coverage* in a publication, you must be willing to stand up to a journalist like the bad guy Drago in *Rocky IV*, and state with confidence, "I will break you." To do less is like betting your paycheck on a professional wrestling match in an untelevised fight. And given that a total of zero big-name media outlets were reviewing my book, I found myself wondering if Allison was taking Steps 3, 4, 5, and 6.

Frustrated, I turned to my kind-hearted agent:

"Dude, I don't think anyone is reviewing my book. Should I call Allison?"

"What for?"

"To ask her if she'll follow up with some of the reviewers."

"You mean actually *call* a reviewer? And say, 'Hey, I sent you a book—hurry up and read it, you mental sloth'?"

"Uh, kinda. Maybe a little less sarcastic."

"Do you know how many books reviewers get each day?"

"Not really."

"Okay, here's a hint: all of them. *Every* book that *every* publisher publishes goes to the same list of a few hundred reviewers nationwide. So the reviewers get about a choo-choo-train boxcar of books every week. Wouldn't that be a fun job? How about if every publisher's publicist called about every book? Would that be helpful? Calling a book reviewer is like shooting them in the ass with a crossbow with a note that says, 'In case the book I sent is actually working its way toward the top of the pile, please move it to the back.'"

"It doesn't matter that I'm special?"

"Oh, you're special all right."

"Do you have any promotional ideas?"

"Yeah. You can hire a radio publicist. She'll want a lot of dough."

"I have three hundred twenty-five dollars, a whistle, some string, and a frog. I think I can get my hands on a slingshot, too."

"I'll email you the gal I recommend. Call her, tell her you're broke, and beg."

"Always the defender of my dignity, you are."

"Hey, Yoda, you want another book deal? Sell books. You wanna sell books? Invest your own money in the deal and hire my friend Audrey. I don't know what else to tell you."

"I feel warm inside just talking with you."

"Eat me."

"Seriously, I think I kind of have a crush on you."

"Then make me happy. Hire Audrey, and let me work."

Hiring Audrey

"Okay," Audrey said. "I'll cut the fee in half, but I'll need you to do all the grunt work. Send out books and stuff like that."

"Deal," I said.

Marketing, hiring people, selling—this being an author thing sucks, I thought.

In case you're wondering, hiring Audrey cost the exact same amount as my advance, ergo my profits at this point equaled … zero. Any first-time author hoping to break through for the long run is going to need to be prepared for this: Your first book is to get you noticed, *not* to make money. When money comes in, spend it on advancing your bookselling cause.

The Wacky World of Radio Interviews

Thanks to today's technology, it's much easier for a publicist to orchestrate the life of a client. Audrey directed me to set up a Google Calendar. The calendar then loiters about in cyberspace, remaining accessible to anyone I choose.

"I want you to fill in the calendar with everything that could make you inaccessible," Audrey explained. "If you have a function, list it. If you have a trip planned, list it. If you go to the bathroom at a particular time, list it. I need to know where you are twenty-four/seven for the next month."

"I'm on it," I said, and I was. Before the day ended, my calendar was posted, and before dinner, Audrey began emailing me radio bookings to add to it. My bride and I were so excited about this newfound route to fame and fortune, we adjourned to the front porch post-dinner for martinis. And as anyone who drinks martinis on a Friday night knows, one isn't enough, two is too many, and three isn't nearly enough.

The phone rang the next morning at 7:15 A.M. Never having received a phone call at that hour on a Saturday, I staggered out of bed to answer; clearly, someone close to me had suffered a tragedy of horrifying scope.

"Yeah?"

"Prioleau Alexander? Hey, it's Gordon Huey, producer for the *Mike in the Morning Radio Show*. Hang on one sec ... Mike's coming out of a break, and you'll be live in ten seconds."

Not good.

"Hey there, Mike's Maniacs, we're back, and we're going to start this hour with Pre-Law Alexander, who has written a hilarious new book entitled *You Want Fries*

With That? A White-Collar Burnout Experiences Life at Minimum Wage. Pre-Law, how are you this morning?

"*Unintelligible.*"

"Great, great ... now, what inspired this book?"

"*Unfunny, garbled response.*"

"And what did you learn from the experience?"

"*Less funny, barely English explanation.*"

"I see. How has it changed you?"

"*Insert the most inane, idiotic crap you can imagine here.*"

"Well, Pre-Law, this has been a really great interview. I can practically hear the economy turning around from the sale of your books!"

I staggered back to bed.

"Who was it?" my wife asked.

"It was my writing career. It called to say good-bye."

Getting It Together

Despite that crushing setback, and with hopes that *Mike in the Morning* wouldn't report me to Audrey, I set about to develop some intelligent, funny answers to the obvious questions that I might be asked. The good news was that I couldn't do worse. The bad news was that I knew, in fact, I could. And probably would.

VIDEO KILLED THE RADIO STAR

My First Radio Performance Gets a Do-Over

It turned out that my radio publicist, Audrey, was awesome. My Gmail inbox flooded with radio interviews, and in short order, I transformed into a Google Calendar wizard. Audrey booked me from sea to shining sea, sometimes as many as five interviews in a day.

Conducting an interview on a book like mine isn't rocket science, because the host can tell what the listeners will want to know once they hear the title. The obvious questions include: What inspired this? What jobs did you do? Which was the worst job? Which was the best? Did you learn anything? In a radio interview, the host is *everything*. If the *host* ain't paying attention, the *listeners* aren't paying attention, and if the host ain't a fan, the listeners won't be fans. Very quickly, I was able to identify the different varieties of hosts:

1. The *they-actually-read-the-book-and-can't-wait-to-ask-questions* host. For a humorist, these interviews are a blast, because you're talking to a new friend. They ask very specific questions, and they laugh at everything you say. This is good because being funny is a hell of a lot easier when the audience *thinks* you're going to be funny. If the host has read the book, the interview is usually peppered with comments like, "People, *go get this book.*"

2. The *their-producer-read-the-book-then-told-them-with-amazement, "It was actually good, this guy is cool"* host. These interviews can be fun, because the host is actually interested in the book and semi-plans to read it; as a result, they ask off-the-cuff questions they want answered prior to beginning the book. These interviews tended to be a little more serious, because they want to know things like, "Did you make fun of your coworkers?"

3. The *didn't-know-who-was-on-the-phone-until-the-producer-handed-them-a-Post-it-with-your-name-and-book-title* host. These interviews are fine, because my weird name and self-explanatory book title made for easy, instant conversation. The vast majority of the interviews fell under this category.

4. The *kinda famous* host. Damn, I say, damn. Every one of these hosts is painful, because these individuals are trying to make the big time— and just want to hear themselves talk for three straight hours; listening to someone else talk takes away from their time. Really, really big-time hosts are professionals, and they conduct interesting interviews, but scrappers on the way up ... not so much. Example: You know that feeling when you are on the phone trying to talk to a friend about an important topic and they are on the other end reading through their email? And about ten seconds into the call, you tell them you gotta run, because they aren't paying attention to you? Yeah, that was my experience with the four kinda famous hosts I spoke with.

Most radio interviews revolved around the questions you would pretty much expect:

HOST: Well, Pree-o-lak, this sounds like a funny book. What inspired it?

ME: I'd been in advertising for about thirteen years, and I reached the burnout point where I was daydreaming about other jobs. I went online and took one of those Professional Personality Profiles that tells you what you should do. When I got through with my likes and dislikes, the only jobs it could find for me were

"Sniper" and "Beer Taster." Then, by the time I got to year fourteen, it was pretty much quit, or take a hostage.

(Insert a few minutes of talking about finances, wife's income, lack of kids, the host's desire to quit sometimes, too. ...)

HOST: What was the best job?

ME: Well, they were all torturous in their own ways, but I'd have to say the best was construction, because the money was decent and you got paid in cash. Money aside, the bennies of being an ice-cream scooper were pretty good.

HOST: Do you get tired of ice cream?

ME: Unfortunately, no.

HOST: So what was the worst job?

ME: Easy. The ER. You know that TV show *Cops*? It's like watching *Cops* in 3D smell-o-vision. The ER is where those people go when they're too sick to beat their wives.

(Insert several minutes of discussion about the other jobs I worked, and the lousy jobs the host worked between firings. Note: Radio people get fired a lot. ...)

HOST: So, Pry-O-Lee-A-You, what did you learn out of all this?

ME: Several things. If you want to avoid going to hell, tip the pizza guy at least a fiver. Never ride a horse in boxer shorts. The words *please* and *thank you* will get you a bigger ice-cream cone. And most importantly, sitting in pointless-but-air-conditioned meetings is a pretty sweet way to pay the bills. No one truly misses air-conditioning and money until they don't have them anymore.

HOST: Anything else you'd like to add?

ME: You bet. Please, please, for the love of everything holy, go buy my stupid book. Your listeners are the thin, thin line between me and working at Home Depot, and I beg you to spare me that. In fact, you *owe* it to me, because y'all are some of the few people in the world who actually read. Get out there and buy! Buy TEN freakin' copies, and give 'em as gifts—use 'em to level tables; I don't give a crap. Buy the book, or I'll triangulate your location like those cops on *Forensic Files*, hunt you down, and put a shank in your ass. Do you hear me, you mouth-breathing cheapskates? Do you??!!

HOST: Well, thanks for being with us today, Prioleau Alexander, author of *You Want Fries With That?* Now, traffic and weather together—

ME: Buy or die, you penny-pinching morons! Buy! Or! Die!

Not Sure Why Video Killed the Radio Star

A television appearance for a newbie author is very rare, and exciting indeed. My publicist, Allison, set me up with a couple of morning TV shows, and my experience on the FOX News affiliate in one of the cities said it all.

I arrived early and was directed to "the green room," where the show's producer would come and fetch me. Now, perhaps you are a high-rolling celebrity and spend lots of time in "green rooms," but this was a first for me. Striding the hallway on my collision course with this famous, symbolic room-of-the-famous caused me a few butterflies, but I swallowed them down.

Good thing, too, because the experience wasn't worthy of so much as a gut-flopping caterpillar. This "green room" was neither green nor lavish, and the only buffet available was behind a Plexiglass snack window at a buck a throw. In fact, it was pretty much a Doc-in-a-Box waiting room, but instead of Norman Rockwell prints on the walls, it had posters advertising FOX TV shows. I scored a package of Oreos, thinking it would get my teeth looking their whitest, and settled in for the wait.

About ten minutes later, the show's producer/director arrived, and sat down next to me:

PRODUCER: You're first name is pronounced Pro-Lowe?

ME: That's close enough.

PRODUCER: Okay. I'm just going to lead you out to the set, and the host, Mike, will interview you. The general rule is two minutes, three minutes if you're great.

ME: I'm shooting for four minutes!

PRODUCER: I like the way you think.

On the set:

MIKE THE HOST: Okay, and coming back *after* the break we have Pro-Lowe Alexander, author of *You Want Fries With That? A White-Collar Burnout Experiences Life at Minimum Wage!*

DIRECTOR: And ... we're *off the air!* Ninety seconds, people.

MIKE THE HOST: You know, Pro-Lowe, I gotta say, this sounds like a great book. I know how you feel. Man, I hated this job for years. Got to the point where I was angry driving into work. I thought about quitting, but—damn, man. House, wife, kids, health insurance, what a nightmare. I went to the station manager and had a sit-down, and he said, "You need to get your mind right." It took a while, but I worked through it. You know?

ME: Sure, I—

DIRECTOR: Ten seconds!

MIKE THE HOST: I got a million questions. Hang on a sec.

DIRECTOR: And four … three …

MIKE THE HOST: We're back with Pro-Lowe Alexander, author of *You Want Fries With That? A White-Collar Burnout Experiences Life at Minimum Wage.* Pro-Lowe, I hear you have an event in our fair city today.

ME: Yes, sir. I'll be at the Alabama Booksmith from six to eight *P.M.*

MIKE THE HOST: Great. Just great. That's an event no one will want to miss. And speaking of miss, here's Miss Katie Phillips with today's weather. (*Pause and a smile for the toss*) Hey, Pro-Lowe, you did great, just great. Thanks for coming by. I really appreciate it.

ME: Thanks.

MIKE THE HOST: The exit is just to your left, over there. You bet. Hey, thanks for coming by. Come back any time.

When Media Was Unsocial

One of the things unavailable back in the old days was serious social media. Believe it or not, there was a time in America's history that didn't include Facebook, Twitter, Instagram, or Ad Words on Google.

Today, as everyone knows, there are billion-dollar industries that simply wouldn't exist without access to these communication channels. Hell, social media is so influential that there are yo-yos who make a living as "influencers," which pretty much means encouraging weak-minded people to make stupid purchases and even stupider life decisions. Back in 2008, we called those people "multilevel-marketing reps," but today people with this "job" actually make money.

Of course, now all of these marketing channels are available and critical. They are what smart and motivated authors use to push their books out to new audiences, and they serve as the lifeblood for authors choosing a small publishing house or the self-publishing route. (They seem to be "free," but that's assuming your time, creativity, and work have no value or cost.) These are all tools that must be mastered, or at least acquired by paying someone else who has mastered them. If you're smart, you can probably hire a teenager to do the work in return for a four-hundred-dollar game console.

That said, these tools and influencers are changing the way citizens of our globe consume and utilize information. As an example, let's consider women's clothing.

Someone like F. Scott Fitzgerald might have written: "Her choice of evening attire spoke of a time lost to the stars, when a woman's dress served to describe her view of the world and her place in it—her love of the arts, her yearning for validation as a successful woman, and her subtle desire to attract the gaze of a man seeking a partner, not an object."

An influencer will write: "Makes my ass look hot."

Yes, fellow creative, the comparison makes you chuckle, but who's garnering the most attention? You, a brilliant writer giving a talk at a bookstore about your thematic novel that explores the struggles, sacrifices, and all-too-rare examples of "pulling oneself up by one's bootstraps," a novel that represents your heart-wrenching exploration of deep issues, based on personal experience, research, interviews, and two years of your life? Or someone on *The View* tweeting during a commercial break, "This book sucks. Bootstrap theory is a lie. It's impossible. A racist white privilege myth! #TruthInaNutshell."

Does this reality cause me despair? All this attention directed toward someone with such a shallow and unimaginative view of the world? There's nothing that can be done about it, so I must simply observe it and accept it. But the truth is that no one watching *The View* buys books anyway. *People* magazine, maybe. Books, no.

You just can't let the morons of the world get under your skin. Our art matters, and it always will. Okay, maybe it's not important to people who follow the hashtag #FunnyFartJokes, but your work as a writer is important. Social media might be dumbing down America at the speed of sound, making it much harder to get your message and thoughts heard, but there still exist people who want to have their minds stimulated, not "influenced." Okay, not many—but some. A few.

Why lie? Social media sucks. I mean, it's good if you have a hot ass and want to drive traffic to your Only Fans page, but first-time authors trying to sell a book to the people who spend more than thirty minutes a day on social media is like trying to sell classical music records to fans of Marilyn Manson.

ON THE ROAD

The Dream Becomes (Un)real

For a struggling author, the idea of being on "book tour" is analogous to what a sixteen-year-old heterosexual male thinks about being in a hot tub with Katy Perry. The thought of it happening sounds like more fun than being a Viking, and you have no idea what you'll do when you get there, but you know in your heart that the experience is going to make you very, very, very happy.

Before going on, however, there's something important you should know about the tradeoffs of the various publishing options:

- Writers securing a deal with a big publishing house enjoy the benefit of the publisher's marketing horsepower and their minor influence with the media, and—if they are lucky—the publisher will plan and pay for a book tour.

- Writers securing a deal with a small publishing house will have the benefit of personal service and a publisher passionate about the writer's individual work—but something like a book tour is most likely going to happen on your own dime. You should note as well that a small publishing house probably has contacts out there in the publishing world, the value of which cannot be overstated.
- Writers choosing the self-publishing route will have neither of the above, but are, for good or for ill, the captain of their own fate. Your royalties percentage is much higher than with a big publishing house, but you've got to be able to look in the mirror and say, "I'm gonna sell some books today, or die tryin'." It's worth noting that dying *is* one of the options.

Anyway, in my rookie-mind's-eye, my upcoming book tour had it all: the "publicist" working behind the scenes, the publisher paying the freight, the booksellers preparing for my arrival, travel to cities where I wouldn't be related by blood to any "fans," all of whom would be in attendance because they wanted to meet *me* ... very heady stuff, indeed. Needless to say, I was ready to light this particular candle. There were readers out there to be charmed and introduced to America's newest humorist, and I certainly wasn't going to become the next P. J. O'Rourke by emailing my friends and family.

Allison put together a three-legged tour for me: First, I would journey to Pittsboro, North Carolina (shout out to their founding fathers for that great name), then Durham, then Charlotte. The following week would be Columbia, South Carolina, then Asheville, North Carolina, then Greenville, South Carolina, then Atlanta, Georgia, and then Birmingham, Alabama. Finally, I'd be Florida-bound.

It was interesting to me that the bookstores I'd be visiting were all smaller, independent outfits. Allison explained that the big-box bookstores move a ton of books, but they don't have a "regular crowd." The smaller indies develop real relationships with hundreds of customers, many of whom come to the store and ask, "What's new? What's good?" Going to such stores for a signing enables you to introduce yourself to the staff, be friendly, and get them to tell folks, "Hey, I met this author. He was a nice guy."

As you've no doubt discovered by now, details bore me, and my writing doesn't include descriptions of oak-lined roads, the smell of jasmine and honeysuckle, or the sounds of bullfrogs as the sun sets over expanses of yellow-green marsh. I don't object to this style of writing; it's just that it's available from so many writers far more talented than I. Because of this, I'll take you on a bird's-eye view of my book tour and highlight the experiences that made me want to laugh, and weep, gnash my teeth, and throw rocks at the stained-glass windows of nature.

A Fancy-Schmancy Book Tour

This is the thing many struggling writers dream about. Because we have no reference point other than the book signings we've been to featuring our favorite author, we assume our own signing will be the same way: people sitting in the audience listening to us wax eloquent, then queueing up in a long line for a moment of our time.

Here's a four-alarm truth blast to my fellow writers: Going on a "book tour" as an *unknown* author can best be envisioned as an arcade game—let's call it *Whack-an-Ego*.

In each new city, you and your dreams pop up into a bookstore: fresh-faced, excited, and naïve. Shortly thereafter, you'll discover that most of the folks who attend your event will be someone you personally invited, or someone who will say, "Hi, (your name)! I'm a friend of (insert mutual friend's name), and he/she told me I just *had* to come and meet you!" *Whack!* "He/she said something about you writing a book!" *Whack!* "I'm not much of a reader myself, but how can I pass up a book signed by a real, live, famous author?" *Whack!* "Make it out to my sister; she reads a lot. She's read every one of the Harry Potter books!" *Whack!* "Great. Now let me get a picture with you so I can prove to (insert mutual friend's name) that I bought a book. He/she would never forgive me if I didn't!" *Whack! Whack! Whack!*

If there's a shining light within the getting-published solar system, it is the opportunity to meet the folks who own America's independent bookstores. It is a well-agreed-upon fact that making money as an independent bookstore owner is damn near impossible, but these people run stores anyway.

As I pressed for the backstory with each of the owners I met, none of them hinted at any sort of bitterness or animosity concerning this business reality—in fact, all the people I met came into the profession with their eyes wide open. The money-seekers, for the most part, ran screaming from the industry when the monster known as Amazon burst onto the scene, revealing the ugly, Walmart-reality of the American consumer: Many have no interest in the environment or experience that comes with a book purchase; they simply want to know the price.

Ernest Hemingway wrote a short story entitled "A Clean, Well-Lighted Place," and although many scholars have analyzed it as a story of hopelessness, I find there to be an undercurrent within it—a theme that says, "The place matters," even to a dying old man filled with despair. There are intangible details within a place that give it a tangible feel, and I believe it's possible the old man in the story is there to absorb the mysterious ambience.

Do such places exist? I think they do. They absorb the energy and dreams and thoughts of those who've been there before you, and breathe them onto you in the time you spend there. In my experience, these places are usually public, yet intimate. Some are finely appointed; some are the proverbial dive; some are loud, some quiet.

This is the realm of cafés, bars, restaurants, ballparks, marinas, front porches, bed-and-breakfast homes ... and independent bookstores. You enter the right one and the words *almost perfect* come to mind, yet you don't know why. These special places have this aura because they *are* this aura. Like a piece of art that truly captures the artist's soul, the place is a reflection of its owner—one of those rare souls who has the gift of putting this here and that there, and providing an exacting ambiance of *realness*. Perhaps, in the parlance of our times, you could say the place has a "feng shui of authenticity."

This, I believe, is the goal of the people who own our country's "indies." At some point in their life, they entered a perfect bookstore environment, and the sentiment of the place seeped into their soul, never to leave. The feeling, the design, the smell of books, the clientele, the curiosity in the air ... together, these intangibles orchestrated an irresistible siren's song and drew these special people into the bookstore-owner fold.

For this reason, they *care* about their store—and every detail within it. They seek to provide book buyers with not just a place to buy books, but also a clean, well-lighted place, where the burdens of life seem far away.

If you have an indie bookstore in your town ... well, use them or lose them. Like you, these are people who love books—not ebooks or audiobooks, but real books you can hold, and smell, and lay on your nightstand. Amazon might deliver to your door and save you a couple bucks, but Amazon will never smile at you, attend church with you, or sit in the same little league stands with you.

Bookstore Employees

If you don't know me, and my breathtaking catalog of human failings, I *can* make a good first impression. That's because of the following reasons:

  a. I think I am *many* things, but "a big deal" is not one of them.
  b. Telling other people about myself is the single most painful topic I can think of, so I'd much rather ask about you.
  c. I tend to smile a lot, which leads you to believe I'm listening to your response.

With that said, I've discovered there are two types of bookstore employees, both of which a traveling author must strive to make a good impression with. First, there is the CUKE employee—and I hasten to add that 90 percent of indie-bookstore employees are CUKEs. *CUKE* stands for Cheerful-Upbeat-Kind-Employee, and it's obvious that they share the owner's vision about the store's sense of place: When you introduce yourself, they make immediate eye contact, smile broadly, and give you a tiny feeling of celebrity.

It is clear that they enjoy having authors visit, and they are at least mildly impressed that the human in front of them made it through the horrifying submission-to-publishing gauntlet. Every single time—and I mean every time—CUKEs take the time to come around from behind the counter, lead you to your spot, and ask, "Can I get you something? Water?" One hundred percent, without fail. This must be because history has taught them that authors are either really health-conscious and focused on hydration, or perhaps hungover. I don't know which. CUKEs are wonderful about hovering, and you can bet that if that your water disappears into your stomach, another will reappear in a jiff.

On the other end of the spectrum are the YAW employees, named for their "You Are Who?" approach to hospitality. When you encounter a YAW, it goes without saying that the owner of the bookstore is not present, and is thus counting on the YAW to make the author feel welcome. They get an F.

The initial meeting with the YAW will follow a very specific, scripted choreography, the picture of which is difficult for a writer of my minimal skills to paint, so bear with me. I'll try.

Envision this: The YAW is doing something very important on the store computer. You approach and stand silently for between thirty and forty seconds. Eventually, the YAW ever-so-fleetingly cuts their eyes to you, granting permission for you to interrupt the vital updating of their Pinterest feed.

You say, "Hi! My name is (insert your name), and I have an event with you today. Just wanted to let you know

I'm here, and to see if there's anything specific you'd like me to do."

The YAW's face will remain expressionless, making sure you think they *don't* know who you are, even though you both know that they know exactly who you are. Said YAW will type one last thing into computer, and—avoiding eye contact—scan behind the counter for the micro-scrap of paper bearing your name.

Upon locating the scrap, which is right where they put it, the YAW will study the scrap, look up at you, offer a smile detectable only by a Sicilian pantomime expert, and says, "Hi, I'm YAW. You'll be sitting at the desk over there. Let me know if I can get you anything."

Aaaaand, We're Off!

When it was time for my very first book signing, my wife, Heidi, and I arrived early in St. Elsewhere, because we'd heard it was an important stop. Besides, when a published author such as myself arrives for an event of such import, there may be need for pre-event adoration and ass-kissery. My public loves me, and I love them, and together we dance lightly across the misty, mystic Never Never Lands of fact and fiction, where time is a lonely hunter.

The bookstore itself was nestled within an idyllic little village atmosphere, more Hobbit Shire than reality. We lunched at an outdoor café, and marveled at the lovingly tended flora that draped the scene: The birds chirped, the breeze blew, and I confess I half-expected our server to be a Munchkin. We dined on the body of a cow that no doubt volunteered itself for consumption, and together we shared cheerful, pithy commentary on the day, the scenery, and the rainbows that streaked across the sky and ended at our feet. I think at one point we laughed until we cried.

Following our luncheon, we stepped across the cobbled courtyard to the site of my event, tastefully choosing not to capture a tacky Kodak moment as we whisked past the sign that trumpeted my impending arrival. The bookstore was perfect in every detail: just the right size, just the right mix of interesting and eclectic books, just the right mix of a melting-pot staff.

Heidi and I chatted with the kind and attentive staff, browsed the books, and smiled as my public assembled. By 2:03, there were twenty-five "fans" sitting on the collective edge of their seats in the speaking area, and I swept into the room with an aplomb normally reserved for Bernie Sanders at a fundraiser.

For the next forty minutes, I wove my tales and showered my audience with a gentle rain of insights and provocation, casting my net of wit and hauling in roars of laughter. My comments inspired bobble-headed agreement, and on a couple of occasions, I stammered as my mind drifted to the mathematics associated with all the upcoming sales.

I took questions, and the answers rolled off my tongue like a mixed-DNA clone of Joe Rogan and Jordan Peterson.

With that, I announced that I would retire to the lobby to sign books.

I thank my Lord in heaven that neither Heidi nor I was in the path of that thundering herd as they stampeded bookless out the door. The Running of the Bulls in Pamplona, Spain, has nothing on what I witnessed—and I know, because I've run with the bulls. Horrified that all my sales were vanishing before my eyes, I bolted from the platform and sprinted at a forty-five-degree angle toward the front of the store—in hopes of, you know, taking down a couple of the weaker members of the herd—but a stand-up rack of self-help books forced me to stutter-step left, and the old bag with the walker used that moment to gather steam. She made it to the handicap ramp and vanished from sight like a winged monkey in pursuit of Dorothy.

Shortly thereafter, we were in the car.

"Remember what Allison said," my wife opined. "It's not about the sales; it's about meeting the store managers and making a good impression on them. And you did—you were gracious and funny and appreciative, and I guarantee all of the employees are going to recommend your book to their customers. The ones who actually purchase books."

I didn't respond as I watched the countryside roll past. Up ahead, I saw the remnants of some sort of animal that had clearly finished second in its game of chicken with a tractor-trailer. I hoped it was a winged monkey.

Vero Beach

On the opposite side of the spectrum was the signing I had in a quaint little coastal town called Vero Beach. Here, I was informed, C-SPAN's *Book TV* would be filming my talk, and there was even a piece in the daily newspaper the day before. As a result, a number of curious book lovers turned out, and I had a crowd of about forty. For a rookie, this is a very, very big deal. I felt drunk on my McFame.

In a stroke of inspiration, and because I was ten minutes early, I went around and introduced myself individually to each person in the crowd. For some reason, everyone thought this was hilarious—I guess because I kept repeating my name and shaking everyone's hand.

This played to my advantage in a big way, because all those people presupposed that my speech would be funny. Believe me, when people think you are going to be funny, it makes public speaking a lot easier. The event went well, and even the film crew seemed pleased.

"I think you're going to get some extra airtime out of this," the cameraman said. "These things are usually pretty boring."

Thus, I would make my national television debut on a show the crew described as "pretty boring." Ka-ching.

Coral Gables

Books & Books in Coral Gables is by any measure one of the greatest places on Earth. This is largely due to the fact that where most bookstores have a foyer, or, well, a front door, Books & Books has a bar. It is impossible to enter the facility without thinking to yourself, "Hey, I might have myself a cold one."

Upon arrival, I met the assistant manager, who, right on cue, asked me, "Can I get you anything? Water? Coffee? *A beer?*"

Well, hello, Books & Books! To say indie bookstores are rare is a gross understatement. To find a place like Books & Books is like running headlong into a leprechaun riding a unicorn.

It took the assistant manager a couple of minutes to find me, because he mistook my war whoop and sprinting exit toward the bar as a signal that I needed to make an emergency trip to the bathroom. When he found me, seated on a barstool and using my tongue to tap the bartender on the shoulder, he understood—and advised the bartender that I would be drinking on the house. With a full forty-five minutes before my talk was scheduled to begin, I tipped the bartender a ten-spot, hoping he'd keep quiet about the inevitable damage to the Miller Lite inventory.

Behind me was an open courtyard, where a musician was playing classical guitar, which offered a very nice ambience to the early evening. The light was going soft and erasing the reality lines of mad dogs and Englishmen, and time reached that evasive flow that comes with being in just the right place at just the right time. From one end of the bar to the other, the patrons all looked like interesting folks—not pompous, not affected, not dull, not boisterous, not ignorant … interesting, like an international arms smuggler who spends weekends volunteering at church.

Thoughtful-yet-conflicted people are usually the most interesting, I think. One of life's real joys is a conversation with a smart person who isn't sure they are right all the time—a person who listens to a new perspective and thoughtfully considers it. One in ten thousand has that gift.

With no one to chat with—and because my brain works in a helter-skelter, ricochet, moto-cross sort of fashion—I went from thinking about people to thinking about books, to readers, to different sorts of readers, to different sorts of books, to the various sorts of people who rarely read books.

What do non-book-readers think about when they are alone? Like, just sitting on the porch, listening to the spin of their world, and they think about … what? An issue concerning the Buffalo Bills' defensive secondary? A piece of gossip about that political candidate they really hate? Whether Oshkosh or Levi's makes better kids' overalls? Do they think about deep stuff at all—the deep stuff authors write about?

I've always thought that being "alone with my thoughts" for any length of time is a dangerous place—mostly because I focus on all the stupid things I've said and done. Which is a lot. Perhaps that's why I write. And read. And drink beer.

Come to think of it, just about everything I do during my waking hours centers around avoiding a collision with the thoughts.

Anyway, the manager eventually came and got me, and the show went on.

Greenville

My book tour event in Greenville, South Carolina, was particularly memorable, first and foremost because it is the city my mum and stepdad called home at the time. I'd enjoyed a couple of really, really successful bookstore events in my hometown of Charleston, and my stepmom had put on a couple of well-attended private signing events in her home in Charleston, so I was excited to be arriving in another town where there'd be a for-sure welcoming reception.

As you know, parents can be pretty amazing. My mom couldn't attend the event, held at the Open Book, because she was participating in Kairos Ministries, a Christian organization that goes into prisons to hold a weekend-long course on Christianity for inmates who are interested. This is no small leap for a woman who graduated from Hollins College, is a past president of the Junior League, and sits on the vestry of one of the largest Anglican churches in the nation. But that's where she was. My stepdad Lee, however, was at the bookstore for the signing, and he, too, is a very cool cat—who just happens to be the headmaster of Christ Church Episcopal

School. They invited friends and served wine and cheese, and made the event very special.

The turnout was amazing, and I confess that I felt a tiny bit of celebrity creeping in … until the signing started.

"Hi, I'm a Bible study friend of your mom."

"Hi, I'm a hiking friend of your mom."

"Hi, I'm a Historic Greenville friend of your mom."

"Hi, I'm a dog-lover friend of your mom."

"Hi, I'm on the vestry with your mom."

"Hi, I'm a master gardener friend of your mom."

"Hi, I used to work for your mom."

"Hi, I work for Lee."

"Hi, I work for Lee."

"Hi, I work for Lee."

"Hi, I fly planes with Lee."

"Hi, I just love your mom.

"Hi, I just love Lee."

Eventually, we ran out of books. And it got me thinking about the importance of a life well-lived. Those lovely people were there not because they cared about me … they loved my mom and stepdad. Keep that in mind when you market your book.

Chicago Signing

At one point, I told my publicist I was going to be in Chicago with my family, so she suggested she set up a signing while I was there. Right on—the foot traffic alone in Chicago would sell a bunch of books, right? The address she provided seemed a little odd, but surely it must be a hotspot for book consumption, right?

At the end of our vacation, while everyone else headed to the airport, my wife and I caught a cab out to the store in the suburbs of Chicago, a few miles away from the bustle of the downtown "Loop." Why we were leaving the place where tens of thousands of tourists were walking, drinking, and looking to spend their souvenir-money, I cannot say. Mongo only pawn in game of life.

The cabbie pulled up to the curbside, and like the celebrities we are, we exited with much ado. I stopped in the bookstore to scout out the staff (YAW versus CUKE) prior to sitting down for a good-luck beer. I did my usual aw-shucks bit:

Me: Hey! My name is Prioleau Alexander, and I have an event here in forty-five minutes.

Cuke Manager: Well, awesome. Thanks for coming. Can I get you some water? Coffee?

Me: Nah, I'm gonna bop down the street and have a beer.

Cuke Manager: Great. Hey, would you like to speak back in the presentation room? Or out here on the floor?

Me: Out here. I'm pretty easygoing about this stuff.

Cuke Manager: Great. Well, I'll see you back here at six.

Me: Six it is!

5:59 P.M., returning from bar

WIFE: Uh, Prioleau?

ME: Yeah, hon?

WIFE: The sign on the door says, "Wednesday, June sixteenth."

ME: Right. Today is the sixteenth.

WIFE: True. But it's *Monday*, June sixteenth.

6:00 P.M., at the counter

ME: Hey, uh, you ... you ... I'm afraid you've got the wrong date on the door.

CUKE MANAGER: Crap!

To plagiarize Dave Barry: I'M NOT MAKING THIS UP.

CUKE manager runs to door, scratches out the word Wednesday *and writes in the word* Tuesday. *He is way too nice of a guy for me to correct him.*

6:15 P.M., inside the store

ME (*to book browser*): Dude! That's an excellent book!

POOR, INNOCENT BOOK-BROWSER DUDE: It does look funny. And I'm in the midst of a career change.

ME: If you buy it, I'll sign it for you.

POOR, INNOCENT BOOK-BROWSER DUDE: You wrote it?

ME: That I did.

Poor, innocent book-browser dude: Uh, I guess I don't have much choice, do I?

Me: You do not.

Poor, innocent book-browser dude: Uh, okay.

Me: Ka-ching!

6:20 p.m.

Browser Chick: Did you say you wrote that book?

Me: That I did.

Browser Chick: Um, why are you here?

Me: I'm here for a speaking event.

Browser Chick: When?

Me: Right now.

Pregnant pause as her eyes sweep the bookstore for someone, anyone, who is around to hear me speak. Pause lasts long enough for the birth of her next comment.

Browser Chick: You can tell me about your book.

Me: Ka-ching!

Atlanta

As a Christian, I believe that from time to time, God defies the laws of nature—physics, time, medicine, what have you. Why He chooses to intercede in our human time and space is not ours to know—and the most painful occasions are not when we witness a miracle, but when we don't. Childhood cancer, freak accidents, birth defects … the list is long of the things that frustrate us. Why doesn't God intercede then?

I have worked through those issues, and have come to answers that satisfy my intellect and faith, but I won't go into them here. They are long and complex, and I doubt seriously that my writing will miraculously convert anyone reading this book. The issues of suffering and miracles are intensely abstract, and it's a walk each person must make on his or her own.

So, why do I bring it up? Because I am writing this section on battery power, sitting in the passenger seat of my car, midway between Greenville and Atlanta. I'm sitting here because my car has a flat, and I'm waiting on AAA; yes, I know how to change a flat, but I prefer not to do so along the side of one of the busiest interstates in the Southeast. The AAA dude will have one of those professional jacks and will accomplish in two minutes what would take me twenty.

So, back to the topic of miracles: About thirty minutes ago, I was happily inbound to my signing event in Atlanta, listening to Skynyrd and smiling inwardly about how well things had gone in Greenville. I went to pass a cluster of cars that were trudging along below the speed limit, when suddenly one of them filled my windshield.

It was most certainly not a "turned on the blinker and merged into my lane" type of encounter, but a "chase scene from *Cops* where the police officer goes to take down the perp" type of encounter. He wasn't there, and then he was three-quarters of the way into my lane, with a collision imminent. Since two-thousand-pound hunks of metal traveling at seventy miles an hour do not play well together, I hit the brakes and prayed that my deceleration would prevent a crash.

It did. Unfortunately, my car lacks antilock brakes and tends to misbehave when any given driver tries to coax it to stop on a dime.

There is a saying among pilots that goes, "What's the first thing you do during an airborne emergency? You fly the frickin' plane." I'm happy to say that that old saying kicked in as I lost control of my car, and I focused hard on containing the situation.

On swerve number three, the wheels found purchase and took me in the direction the car was headed—which happened to be into oncoming traffic. I recall very distinctly thinking, "Thank God this interstate has those cables across the median."

I knew the cables would rip the car's side to shreds, but anything would beat slamming head-on into the busy Sunday traffic screaming north on I-85.

At this point, I struggle to find an appropriate analogy, because it's difficult for me to capture the nuance of the moment. So, for lack of a more creative mind, I tell you that a barrier of Lincoln Logs and dental floss would have done a better job of slowing me down and redirecting my trajectory than those highway cables did. In fact, I recall thinking "Wow" as I plowed over the steel cables, amazed that they failed to even slow me down, much less redirect my flight. I crossed the median into oncoming traffic as easily as one might take an exit ramp in search of a restroom and a Mountain Dew.

This is when the miracle transpired.

I was now traveling south in the northbound lane, still wildly out of control. In front of me was an eighteen-wheeler, bearing down like, well, a freaking eighteen-wheeler. I did the math in my head, and thought these exact words: "We cannot miss each other, so this is how I will die. Wow, I can't believe this is it. I never thought it would be in a car accident. I wonder if it will hurt?"

I pulled to the right, hoping he would hit me mid-vehicle instead of head-on. He pulled to his right, apparently thinking the same thing … and we missed each other.

Not only did we miss each other, but there was no traffic around him. As a result, we missed, and there were no other cars present to cream me. I simply pulled onto the median, pointing the wrong way, and said, "God, I don't know what you have planned for me, but I hope I'm successful in accomplishing it. You just bent the laws of physics on my behalf, and I'm as sure of that as I am that my hands are going to start shaking in a minute."

I got out of the car and spent several minutes thanking the tractor-trailer driver for being alert, and talking (quite civilly) with the guy who'd cut me off, who had actually stopped to assume responsibility. The cutter-offer called the South Carolina Highway Patrol to report the incident, and I got back in my car to await the trooper.

As I sat there, I offered some prayers of thanksgiving to God for sparing me and to let Him know I'd try to fulfill whatever mission He had in store for me. Then I turned on the radio. The station was playing "Angel" by Sarah McLachlan. I wouldn't believe me either, so there are no hard feelings if you think I'm lying.

Finally, the trooper arrived, took the report, and cleared us all to leave. I was two and a half hours late for my event at A Cappella Books in Atlanta, and the bookstore owner was a complete gentleman about it. To show my appreciation for his understanding and genuine concern, I went out to the car, retrieved my shattered bumper from the backseat, signed it, and left it as a souvenir.

Now I Lay Me Down to Sleep

Being on book tour involves staying in a lot of hotels, with a lot of time to kill. Never having had a job in sales, this hotel life was new to me. Ninety-nine percent of the hotels where I'd stayed in my life revolved around a vacation event, and a good vacation involves as little time spent in the hotel room as humanly possible. On tour, I mostly stayed in the room, as the autograph and selfie seekers just wore me out. A lot of attractive ladies were hurling themselves at my feet—and I'm married. It was best to just stay in the room eating Cheetos and watching that soothing painter dude.

I did, however, remember to take notes on the experience, and here are a few of the nuggets of wisdom I raked in.

The $125 Rule

For some reason, $125 dollars is the exact price point at which you transition from "dump" to "decent." Less than $125 per night, and the person at the front desk will be in civilian clothes, looking like they are on their third straight meth-fueled shift. $125 and up, and you'll enjoy a pleasant conversation with a uniformed person who doesn't seem to hate you.

$125 is the point where straight shower curtain rods give way to those curved "arc" rods, which enable you to shower without the curtain clinging to your skin every time you reach for the soap. It is the magical point where vending machines are displayed without gunmetal fencing between you and your healthy dining experience. Wireless internet appears in your room, not just in the lobby. The air-conditioning units have temperature options beyond "off" and "arctic." Do-not-disturb door hangers are available, and housekeeping resists the urge to beat on your door like Paul Revere at seven *A.M.* The lobby smells like a lobby, instead of curry or microwaved-and-burnt popcorn. Towels look like towels, instead of sheets. And accommodations are made for those newfangled technologies that demand a power source in order to recharge.

Sadly, I didn't come to this realization until the end of my book tour, and by then, I'd already stayed in the cheapest places several times to save my publisher money.

Hotel Room Television

If there was a bright spot to being on book tour, cable television was it. My wife and I live out in the sticks and get our TV through rabbit ears and tin foil, so imagine my joy at discovering fifty-plus channels for my viewing pleasure. Boy, had I fallen out of touch with my beloved country! I learned hundreds of new things, among them:

- Basketball players are no longer required to dribble.
- Parents who allow their under-eighteen children to go into acting or entertainment should simply cut to the chase and sell them into child-slavery prostitution rings, thus saving all that time needed for auditions.
- Whoopi Goldberg represents "black people" in the same way Larry the Cable Guy represents "white people," yet the big media outlets breathlessly report on her every drooling remark.
- The only promise that appears off-limits to people running for president is "eternal life, through me." Claiming, however, that "I am the truth, and the way, and the life" is apparently acceptable.

- If a nature-based TV channel is doing a show on lions, you will pull for the lion to catch the impala. If the documentary is on impalas, you'll pull for the impala to escape.
- A thing called Ultimate Fighting has revealed that all the movie fight sequences we Americans love so dearly are totally fake. Among true, highly trained bad-asses, a fight consists of two punches, then one guy choking the other.
- On TV dramas, we love cops. On TV news, we don't love cops. Translation: We love cops as long as they aren't really cops.
- The rules for parenting are no longer passed along from mother to daughter and father to son. They are doled out in ten-second blurbs between sitcoms by actors and sponsored by media conglomerates that "care."
- Every cell-phone carrier believes that the carrier I subscribe to is a call-dropping, overpriced, family-unfriendly, no-network rip-off. Which is a pretty good description of every cell-phone service I've ever subscribed to.

When I wasn't watching TV while on book tour, I was alone with my thoughts. And the ghosts that haunt every writer. Every now and then, I'd have very productive conversations with myself:

VOICE: What are you doing?

ME: I'm writing.

VOICE: Well, obviously. Why are you writing? Why aren't you walking the strip drinking beers? You're in frickin' Daytona Beach at the beginning of summer. Go have some fun!

ME: I need to write.

VOICE: That makes no sense. You're on book tour.

ME: I still need to write.

VOICE: Great writers take huge breaks between books. To, you know, recharge their batteries. Get a new perspective.

ME: Someday I'll do that.

VOICE: Do it now.

ME: I can't.

VOICE: Why? You're scared?

ME: Say what?

VOICE: *I said*: Are you scared?

ME: Scared of what?

VOICE: You are! Ah-ah-ah ... you're scared that you don't have another book in you.

ME: Don't be ridiculous. Writing comes easy to me.

VOICE: Yes, copywriting does ... but you ain't writing another real-estate brochure here, are you? You can knock that crap out with your eyes closed, but this *book* thing has you spooked. I can smell it on you.

ME: Back off. God opened a door, and I'm walking through it. I'll keep walking until the door closes.

VOICE: Yes, yes—trying to shut me up with the Christian thing. Well, *Reverend* Alexander, if you're such a Christian, why are you drinking beer while you write?

ME: Easy, there. Jesus's first miracle was turning water into wine.

VOICE: Right. *Wine.* At a *wedding.* It wasn't turning water into cheap watery beer so he could drink it alone. In a hotel room.

ME: Cut me a break, man. I'm a frickin' wreck here. I have no idea if my book is selling. No idea if I'm going to make a dime on this whole stupid dream. I'm probably wearing my friends out asking them to help me sell the book. I've been away from my wife for two weeks. I thought getting published would be some sort of mental release, and so far it's just as frustrating as *not* being published. I want to turn off my brain, get it freakin' rewired, and be an accountant.

VOICE: Wait here. I'm gonna run out and see if I can find someone in this area code who feels sorry for you. I'll see if I can track down a whaaa-mbulance while I'm out.

A Little Nugget of Advice

I often encourage writers to move outside their preferred genre and play around with different concepts. Hell, just crafting impressive emails at work can give you some fine practice, and certainly impress your recipients.

For example, let's say you want to indicate that the team needs to do some research on a topic. Give that sentence some flair: *We need to dig down into this like a terrorist digging his foxhole when a squadron of F-16s appears over the horizon. We need to know this topic like a Big Pharma lobbyist on the way to the Capitol to buy a law. We need to crush our way through this project like a congressman smashing his way through a crowd to an open bar.*

Try it. It's fun.

One of the items that popped into my head while channel-flipping in that hotel room, was some advice for my nephews. One was headed to college, and one was graduating college. As my wife and I don't have kids, our nephews' and nieces' well-being is as far as our parental instincts go. Young people are far too brilliant to ask their parents for advice, but since I'm an uncle, every few years, I'll offer a suggestion they find to be almost acceptable. Not, smart, of course, but kinda-sorta-maybe worth adhering to. I turned off the TV, sat down with my laptop, and wrote a couple of letters.

To my nephew headed to college, I emailed:

So, here you go, young man headed to college. Take the following advice like it's emitting from a burning bush. I realize you won't, of course, but a few years from now, we can drink some beer and laugh about all the dung heaps you ended up in because you didn't.

Ready?

Seniors at college will look like grown men—wise and experienced veterans, capable of dispensing important insights on life. They aren't. If you have a question more important than which Zippy Marts accept fake IDs, call your dad.

Speaking of fake IDs, avoid bars. They are expensive, illegal for anyone under 21, and tend to attract guys who want to fight (and girls who want to be fought over). Push, shove, swing— there goes your scholarship. That's a call to your dad you don't want to make.

In planning for fall semester, sign up for later classes—it's cold at 8:00 A.M. In the spring, sign up for early classes—when it warms up, you'll want to be outside.

In high school, you attended classes and played sports from about 8:00 A.M. until 3:00 or 4:00

P.M. If you can force yourself to maintain that schedule, and view college as a "job" from 8:00 A.M. to 4:00 P.M., you'll crush it. You'll be amazed when other people flunk out.

Nothing, and I mean nothing, good happens after midnight. After 1:00 A.M., the police start getting involved. After 2:00 A.M., it's the ER. Regardless of your classmates' preferred schedules, have your fun earlier, and be counting sheep when the cops start pulling out the tasers and pepper spray. If you must stay out late, use this rule of thumb: When the clock strikes midnight, think about what you want to do, then do the opposite.

Speaking of cops, there will be times in the next four years when you will feel called to "reason" with them—perhaps in your own defense, or for a friend who's crossed the line. This is a mistake. Cops are not reasonable people after 6:00 P.M. Until you are 40, the only words you should ever say to a cop are, "Yes, sir," and "No, sir," and "I'm happy to comply, officer."

Along those same lines, college professors are fairly predictable, too. In all liberal arts classes, sit in the front row, nod a lot, ask questions, and—this is key—whenever you are answering a short answer or essay question, be a human parrot.

When writing your answer, focus on the question: "What does the guy grading my test want to hear?" As an added benefit, this will be good training should you choose to pursue a career in corporate America.

I'd also encourage you to avoid taking advantage of the fact that most college profs don't care if you come to class. The only reason for missing a class is if an ER physician is standing over you, holding paddles and yelling, "Clear!"

The most tireless, obsessed, mean-spirited humans on the planet are not radical terrorists—they are meter maids on college campuses. You have been warned.

Make sure your iPod has Andrea Bocelli's Romanza *on it. The chicks will think you are cool and mysterious. If you can stand it, have some jazz, too.*

If your school has a foreign language requirement, remember that the vocabulary words you learn are considered fair game in later semesters. Don't kill the brain cells containing those words.

At Auburn, where I went to college, riding a bicycle was considered "driving." You might want to check on the local laws in your new township.

Sitting around with friends at the library, laughing, texting, or flirting with girls doesn't qualify as studying. Sure, that may seem obvious— but you're about to encounter thousands of people who can't grasp that concept.

You will meet a lot of kids who do recreational drugs. I implore you not to go down that road. Ever heard of an employer insisting on a drug test? Do you know what can prevent you from obtaining a security clearance? Yes, the real world takes recreational drug use WAY seriously, despite what movies may suggest otherwise. Make your own decisions regarding beer, but draw a line in the sand with drugs—and seek a reputation as someone who thinks drug users are geeks. You'd also be wise to avoid "trying dip": I did not, and 35 years later I'm still a nicotine addict.

You will also meet a lot of kids who bet on football. To that, let me say this: Gambling is the surest way to lose everything. Think about it: If Tiger Woods tried to blow all his money on drugs, alcohol, and partying, he couldn't—because he'd be dead before the money ran out. But gambling? He could lose it all in a week. He could lose it all, plus enough more to have a bookie break his legs. Think about it before you get a taste of the "easy money" that comes with a few innocent bets.

If you want to join a fraternity, don't join one that hazes pledges. Although the Marine Corps might haze recruits on their way to becoming Marines, it's necessary. A fraternity is a beer-drinking club—and hardly worthy of demanding some sort of silly trial by fire that can scar or even kill you. Along those same lines, if you join the Marines, feel free to get a tattoo. Fraternity tattoos, however, are just sad.

You're also going to encounter lots of kids from different economic backgrounds—there will be rich kids with their parents' credit cards, and there will be kids who are working their way through school without a dime from their folks. Don't be quick to judge either—you'll meet good people in both categories. Just don't try to run with the rich kids, because their parents' credit cards aren't yours. Along that same vein, don't pressure your less fortunate friends to do stuff that costs money, unless you're going to pick up the tab.

Remind yourself how blessed you are: Put an index card on your mirror that says, "Today, someone my age, who couldn't afford college, may die serving in the military."

At this point in your life, you have no idea what's at stake regarding your college years—but it's a lot.

The choices you make in college will impact the rest of your life. The Golden Rule should guide you in your personal relationships on campus, especially when it comes to dating. You are not living in a bubble where all is forgotten after you get your diploma.

You won't believe how quickly the "real world" will pigeon-hole you into the career you choose, which will likely be based on your major. If you sleepwalk through college, the world doesn't mind—the world doesn't even care.

That's because as much as the world needs engineers, businesspeople, marketers, teachers, warriors, doctors, and nurses, it also needs ditch-diggers. Lots and lots of ditch-diggers. This is your one four-year window to explore the buffet of professions. Talk to peers, adult professionals, professors, and ditch-diggers to see what their lives are like, and find a passion to pursue.

College won't go by fast, but it will go by—and when you pop out on the other side, the world will only be your oyster if you know where oysters grow, have a boat to find them, have the tools to harvest them, and have the know-how to crack one open.

Remember this: The world and technology have changed more during your 12 years in school than *it changed in the previous 1,000 years. The job where you'll spend your career might not even exist yet. Old dudes like me can't help you with this—I come from a generation that could never figure out how to stop the 12:00 on the VCR from blinking. You and you alone need to survey the ice and skate to where the puck is going to be. Oh, and go to church. Believe it or not, God goes to college with you.*

To my nephew graduating from college, I sent this letter:

Well, well, well … off into the real world. Allow me to offer a little advice.

First, the biggie: If your salary is, say, $50,000, understand you are now living in the horrid reality of "gross" versus "net." The government takes a huge chunk, and you're going to have to pay for car insurance, car repairs, property taxes, phone and internet access, food, clothing, shoes, rent, utilities and, perhaps, health insurance. You don't know it, but in college you lived like a millionaire. Now you are broke, and need to be prepared for it.

You do not need a new car.

You do not need a new computer.

Do not get or use a credit card.

Do not get an apartment by yourself, no matter how much you think you "deserve" it. Roommates divide up the bills. Along this same vein, do not buy a new TV, a new sound system, a new gaming system, or new furniture. One of the dummies you move in with will already have done this for you.

Do not let the amount of stuff you own exceed what you can put in your vehicle. Once this occurs, you don't own the stuff—it owns you.

Save some money for one good vacation. With a total of one or two weeks off for the entire year, you're gonna need to do something fun. If you put a vacation on a credit card, you have the maturity and intelligence of a six-week-old Irish setter.

Buying a home is not an investment; it is a lifestyle choice. If you enjoy spending every weekend fixing stuff around the house, go for it. If you want to do something else on the weekend, rent.

If you rent, you are not "throwing money away." You are paying for a roof over your head and *an insurance policy that allows you to sleep like a baby knowing you don't have to pay to replace the recently exploded hot-water heater. Or anything, for that matter.*

Here is what your boss and your company owe you: nothing. Anything they give you beyond a paycheck is a blessing. If by some miracle your company offers a matching retirement program, max it out ... no matter how badly it affects your weekend fun.

Unless you are in a drawer with a tag on your toe, do not miss a day of work your first year. If you think you're going to cough up a lung, wear a lung-colored shirt. You can consider calling in sick after a year.

If you get a DUI in the first five years of your employment, sell everything and join the French Foreign Legion. You have just ruined the rest of your life.

During the first few years of work, know that snow skiing, skydiving, snowboarding, rock climbing, and motorcycle riding are done at your own peril. Unless you can add value to your company the day after shattering your hip, missing work for fun-related injuries is considered "extremely poor judgment" by most bosses. Managers don't believe in YOLO.

Do not post anything political or even mildly offensive on social media until you are older. No, it's not fair, but you live in a brave new world.

You are young and expendable ... one day your views will evolve and change, and an internet post lasts forever. It's also worth noting that potential employers will scour your social media before hiring you.

Every email you send will, one day, be read by the person you wrote it about.

Make sure when replying to a text it's not CCed to other recipients.

Say "Yes, sir" and "No, ma'am" to everyone your age or older.

Leave your personal phone in the car and check it during lunch.

Within a year, you will wonder how your company ever got by without you. If you want to find out, start voicing that opinion.

I want to tell you about women, so here's what I know: nothing. Good luck.

Tips are now 20 percent.

Ask every person you know about their car mechanic. When someone loves their mechanic so much that they get choked up discussing the topic, you've found your new mechanic.

Own a gun, and keep it in your bedroom. Get trained on it. You can keep it in a touchpad safe if you want to. If you hear someone in your house, don't "check it out." Stay in your room with you and your lady's back to a corner. Call 911. If someone does come into your room, rest assured they aren't there to negotiate.

You never knew this, but going to the dentist costs money. Do it anyway. Along those same lines, people with bright white teeth look successful. Pay your dentist to professionally bleach yours.

Write thank-you notes for gifts, meals, condolences, and kind gestures. Email does not qualify. Be a grown-up and get some stationery with your name on it, then use it. You cannot imagine the positive impression it will make on those older than 40.

Taking your lunch to work all year will buy you an all-expense-paid trip for you and your lady-friend to a four-star resort in Mexico. Do the math and you'll find I'm right.

Do not get married without serious premarital counseling; there are lots of issues you haven't discussed or thought through. Also, don't marry for money—you can borrow it cheaper.

Join AAA and carry jumper cables in your car. A basic tool kit isn't a bad idea, even if you don't know how to use it. Someone lending a hand might need them.

Read the essay "A Message to Garcia." Print it out. Reread it 1,000 times. Get it tattooed on your arm if it helps. Then live it.

Put a photo of the American flag on your bathroom mirror. Each day when you see it, say a prayer for the young men and women in our military.

Finally, make sure you have fun, lad. Life is not a dress rehearsal, and you're now on the stage.

I enjoyed thinking through the topics, then writing it down. And it was good practice.

Oh, and in case you're wondering, the answer is "yes and no." The headed-to-college nephew ignored all my advice, and the following summer said he wished he'd followed every word. The real-world-bound nephew did follow my advice, and he thanks me regularly.

It's true: Youth is wasted on the young, and wisdom is wasted on the old.

CAN YOU COMPRESS THAT INTO A TWEET?

Our world, it seems, is moving away from books as a form of entertainment, and this does not bode well for all of us who dream of a career in the lonely art. The real truth be known, our world is moving away from words themselves—anyone seeking the truth in that statement need only look to the delightful world of advertising: One of the founding fathers of modern advertising, David Ogilvy, achieved fame and fortune by providing consumers with detailed information in a way that was interesting and fun to read. His famous Rolls-Royce "clock ad" had somewhere in the neighborhood of seven hundred words of copy. Today? Hell, a twenty-page brochure wouldn't have seven hundred words of copy in it. People like pictures, because words tend to "inform" and "educate," and looking at a picture doesn't demand all that unnecessary thinking.

If we the people are going to drift away from great books because they are filled with too many words, are we also doomed to lose the creative and challenging concepts that writers strive to help us understand? Would it be possible to somehow boil down brilliant literary achievements like Victor Hugo's fourteen-hundred-page *Les Misérables* and still salvage its message for those folks simply too busy to read it? Could, in fact, entire books be reduced to a text message? After thinking through some of the more famous books in my library, I decided they could—and went to work on a cocktail napkin. Let's see ...

Catch-22: Bureaucracy sucks.

Zen and the Art of Motorcycle Maintenance: Beauty is only skin deep.

The Count of Monte Cristo: Revenge is a dish best served cold.

Don't Stop the Carnival: No matter where you go, there you are.

Les Misérables: There ain't no free lunch.

The Great Gatsby: You always want what you can't have.

A Farewell to Arms: Life sucks.

The Sound and the Fury: What goes up must come down.

Atlas Shrugged: Government sucks.

The Hitchhiker's Guide to the Galaxy: 42.

Heart of Darkness: There's a thin line between Saturday night and Sunday morning.

The Screwtape Letters: Satan sucks.

Lonesome Dove: Actions speak louder than words.

Lord of the Flies: Humans suck.

Cold Mountain: Life goes on.

And let's close with a look at the world according to McCarthy:

Blood Meridian: Hell is where you're headed …

The Border Trilogy: Unless, against all odds, you redeem yourself.

No Country for Old Men: Not that it matters.

The Road: Or does it?

If this is where intellectual thought is headed, we should all be very excited about it. You and I are the ones mentally pondering life's deep questions, and perhaps one day in the future we'll be paid handsomely as advertising writers to coax Americans into specific Only Fans sites using our mastery of concepts like "heaving breasts." Or to tweet deep stuff for stupid politicians who want to seem, well, less stupid. Maybe there's a gold mine just below the surface of Instagram posts. Who knows? Hemingway

wrote a story in six words: *Baby shoes for sale. Never used.*
Why not you and me?

Heaving breasts available. Bring some money.

DON'T FEED THE TROLLS

Can You Feel the Love?

As a first-time author, you get to wondering how things are going out there: Is the book selling, is anyone reviewing it, is anyone even commenting on it? The easiest way to find out what's what is simply to google your own name. So I did. I typed: "Prioleau Alexander," then a space, then "book review."

The reviews drifted out over time, and it was really exciting. People who'd never met me loved my writing, and it was the "validation" that all writers dream of as they strive for publication. I did, however, receive one bad review. The title of the review? *Supersize this, Bitch.*

Huh? That doesn't sound so good. But I read on.

And there, squeezed into a mere thousand words, was the angriest "book review" I've ever read. People, I'm talking *venom*—venom the likes of which I've not seen since Sean Penn published his "Open Letter" to the guys who wrote and directed *Team America*. (Great film, BTW. They portray Sean Penn as the putz that he is.) Allow me to pass along some of the reviewer's finer points, along with my response. Prior to beginning, please allow me to again plagiarize the trademark Dave Barry comment by saying, I AM NOT MAKING THIS UP:

REVIEWER: … he manages only to skim the surface of the drudgery of minimum-wage employment.

ME: Gee, I wonder why. Delving *deep* into "drudgery" sounds like it would make for fun reading!

REVIEWER: … there is no discussion of the fact that *somebody* will always have to cook and serve the fast food or clean up the ER when people bleed all over the place, and those somebodies (*sic*) deserve a better quality of life.

ME: I didn't feel the need. That topic is covered endlessly, day after whiny day, by tenured intellectuals, the media, and unpaid book reviewers.

REVIEWER: A good portion of each chapter is dedicated to the history of the product or service involved, but seriously, the question of who actually invented ice cream has nothing to do with the plight of the employee doing the scooping.

ME: Good point—and advice I might well heed if I wrote a book entitled *The Plight of the Minimum-Wage Worker*, which it so happens I did not.

REVIEWER: It's a series of mildly amusing anecdotes and totally unfunny fat jokes. ...

ME: The reviewer is fat.

REVIEWER: It's like if Ted Nugent learned how to write and kept a journal detailing all the things he didn't understand about real life.

ME: I'd buy the hell out that book. Probably give it as Christmas gifts, too.

REVIEWER: Being bored and overpaid is a privilege, not a condition.

ME: Actually, being bored and overpaid is a result; being whiny, passive-aggressive, and a more-compassionate-than-thou phony is a condition.

REVIEWER: I want the first person who sees this guy to punch him in the face.

ME: Aaaand ... cut! This is a review comment I'm not familiar with. But good advice, nonetheless. I think it's always wise for bookish, pear-shaped bloggers to punch former Marines in the face every now and then. Just to keep the pecking order straight.

Why has the internet made so many people mean? Bone-deep mean? I'm sure people feel free to attack and troll other individuals because they are hidden behind their computer screen, but the anger behind the impulse is a mystery.

I've been on mission trips to Ukraine, where I've encountered hundreds of people in small villages who live in hard squalor and eat pickles as a meal. So, why are these internet trolls so unhappy? I mean, other than the fact that the average internet troll is a fat, coddled, entitled, lazy, nose-ringed, neck-tattooed, unemployed asshat?

But Will It Happen to You?

It seemed to me there was a lot of venom inspired by the title of my book. I say the title, because dozens of people attacked me without ever having read the book.

As an experiment, I went to Amazon and researched the work of nonfiction humorists who've achieved what I have not—namely, financial and commercial success: P. J. O'Rourke, David Sedaris, Eric Weiner, A. J. Jacobs, Dave Barry. I figured *one* of these famous writers would be immune from these shrieking toads, either because they were:

- David Sedaris, to the left on the political spectrum;
- P. J. O'Rourke, to the right; or
- just having fun, like Weiner, Jacobs, and Dave Barry.

I mean, hell, all a humorist is trying to do is entertain their audience, and maybe make them think a little, right? I may have virtually nothing politically in common with David Sedaris, but that doesn't mean he's not funny as hell, right?

Apparently ... wrong. Humorists inspire *great* passion among their critics, the harshest of whom take mastodon-sized pains to use sesquipedalian words in order to simply pronounce the writer's work unfunny. (You would be amazed at all the creatively huffy ways a critic can proclaim a harmless joke to be offensive.) Amazon critics, in addition, love to give examples of why these incredibly successful authors aren't funny.

Oh, and please note—I wrote this back when dinosaurs roamed the Earth, and #MeToo, Cancel Culture, BLM, and LGBTQ+ weren't controlling the narrative from sea to shining sea. You get a book published these days? Either don't do internet searches for your reviews, or put on a helmet and some Depends before reading them.

But what, I wondered, would be a book so "good" that all the world would gather around it, hold it aloft, and, uh, at least not bitch about it? Could something *intellectual* achieve such praise? Something *idealistic*? Something *artistic*? Something that resonated with *truth and insight*? Perhaps something *brutal and blunt*? Is this even possible? Every writer wants every reader to be pleased with their work, regardless of the writer's level of success or fame.

No, writers *don't* expect every reader to agree with their ideas, but they do hope to craft their ideas in such a way that the readers will think, "He/she does make an interesting point there." Is this even possible?

I glanced over my library and took note of some of my more treasured hardcover titles. As an English major, I recognize that some of the books I own are over my head and would require an academic coach for me to truly understand, but I've read them all with the belief that they hold some of life's truths and beauty and pain and ugliness. I may not get the nuanced layers of insight, but I can push myself to understand the ideas the writer is exploring. I can enjoy the author's approach to wordsmithing. I can seek to find what writers smarter than I have discovered.

With this in mind, I decided to test a few of the titles against the Amazon critics, and see how they fared. I chose them not because they were my personal favorites, but because they were the ones I would be hardest pressed to challenge standing in front of the English professors at my alma mater. And thus, the experiment began. ...

Here, I will list the title and author of each book, followed by some comments from reviewers.

Breakfast of Champions, **Kurt Vonnegut, Jr.:**

Out of two hundred fifty reviews, nineteen people gave it one or two stars. One decried this classic to be "heavy-handed, smug, obnoxious, and fatuous." Another fan crowed that it was "a nonsensical stream of consciousness dribble."

Sorry, Kurt. I'd like to say, "Maybe next time," but you are, of course, dead.

To Kill a Mockingbird, Harper Lee:

Out of more than seventeen hundred reviews, ninety people gave it one or two stars. Among these reviews, one opined: "fifty pages of good writing and the rest is garbage." Another wrote, "Halfway through the book I was just wishing a bunch of mockingbirds would fly in and end everyone's misery (mine included)."

Uh, Harper? About that Pulitzer Prize …

Lonesome Dove, Larry McMurtry:

Out of three hundred seventy-seven reviews, fourteen gave it one or two stars. But, oh my—what stars! One reviewer from Chicago claimed it was "the worst book I've ever read," and another declared it a "generic, unimaginative piece of crap. Pulitzer Prize … what a joke!"

Larry, perhaps you and Harper can save on postage by sending your Pulitzers back together in one of those flat-rate envelopes they offer at the post office. I know you're dead and all, but perhaps a relative can do it for you?

1984, George Orwell:

Out of well over thirteen hundred reviews, sixty-one proclaimed the book worthy of only one or two stars. One of Orwell's "fans" declared him "a second-rate hack who profiteered on the worst fears of modern man. Today, his book is the modern bible of the paranoid, disgruntled white male."

I don't know about all that—I just want someone to make 1984 fiction again.

It Will Happen to Us All

That, I suppose, is the lesson all first-time authors should take from my own experience with review trolls. No matter how sensitive and kind and politically correct you are, your book will still inspire a volatile reaction from some number of jerks. But why does this surprise me? Why did I think my book could tread some sort of thin line between the internet trolls and haters? Because I'd never had a book published, and it never dawned on me to read the negative reviews on Amazon.

Why would someone invest several of the precious, irreplaceable minutes they have on this planet writing a lousy review on Amazon? In fact, let's chase that rabbit down the hole a little further: Why in the name of all that's holy would someone bother to finish a book they didn't like?

I've read hundreds of books since graduating from college, and here's how many crappy books I've finished: zero. If the book is not good, I stop reading it. Problem solved. Why? Because I am not a paid, professional book reviewer, and thus, it is not part of my job description to plod through writing I don't like. Books are supposed to make you happy/sad/think/wonder/excited/smarter, not bitter.

Hey, I'm all about putting on your big-boy pants and reading the thoughts of those you disagree with … that's how new ideas are formed and common ground is discovered. To that end, I bought one of Al Franken's books a while back, because I wanted to see what he was all about. After two chapters, I discovered all I needed to. The book went to the library, and I managed to go on with my life. At no point did it even dawn on me to continue reading the book so that I could give Al "the business" via a poor review on Amazon. What would be the point?

Sadly, I think I know.

I once had a professor at Auburn who shared Gore Vidal's famous quote: "It is not enough to succeed. My friends must fail." The class laughed, and I waited for him to put the words into their comedic context.

"It's funny," the prof said, "because it's true, isn't it? That tiny, tiny, good feeling you get when something bad happens to someone else? Because it didn't happen to you?"

Some of those in class nodded in bemusement.

True? Sure, it's true—if you're a sick, twisted bastard with enough self-esteem issues to fill a dozen psychiatry textbooks. I understand the amusement of a specific person you dislike failing, but people in general?

The idea that this belief haunts the minds of some percentage of the population makes me think that perhaps Cormac McCarthy does have it right: Perhaps we *are* damned. Perhaps we are little more than a band of spiritual Indians, hopelessly existing on desolate, sun-bleached plains, awaiting the arrival of McCarthy's character "the Judge," who, along with his band of psychopaths, will scalp us of our last remaining hopes of goodness.

My editor noted that this section about trolling might be a serious buzzkill for other writers. I considered this with great discernment, but my point in writing this tome is to level with writers about the things they will experience. And when it comes to trolling, you *will* experience this, and it *will* bother you. It shouldn't, but it will.

Haters gonna hate—but you are an artist, and you must remember that in the realm of art, the dogs bark, but the caravan rolls on.

A TRULY SUCCESSFUL AUTHOR

Tim Dorsey

If you haven't read any of the novels by my Auburn classmate Tim Dorsey, put him on your list. As a crime-humor novelist exploring the insanity of life in South Florida, he is in my top six fiction novelists in modern America—a list I complete with Carl Hiaasen, Christopher Moore, the late Pat Conroy, the late Douglas Adams, and the late Terry Pratchett. Yes, these writers *all* include humor in their writing, but that's why I rank them so highly: They are novelists *and* humorists, a combination of skills that both evades me and holds me in awe.

The story of how I met Tim during college is pretty typical. After dropping off my girlfriend at her dorm following a Tri Delt sorority social, it occurred to me exactly how hammered I was, and I decided it would be a good idea to park my beloved '65 Mustang (The Shark), and stagger the rest of the way back to the KA house on foot.

As I worked my way past the Chi O dorm, a face came into view, walking toward me. I *knew* the face. I knew the face. I knew the—then it struck me: It was Tim Dorsey, the guy who wrote a column for our school newspaper, *The Plainsman*. Prior to reading Tim's column, I didn't know that out-loud laughter could be generated by the written word. Stand-up comics? Sure. But prose? Not witty or cute, but laugh-out-loud funny? I just didn't know there was such a thing. And here he was. Walking toward me. A great writer in the making. I had to tell him I was a fan. Had to. So I said the most intellectual thing I could come up with.

"Holy crap!" I shouted. "You're Tim Dorsey!"

I think I was his first full-volume fan, and it scared him a bit. Also, this was the Big Hair 1980s, and I had a Marine ROTC haircut, at that point shared only by fans of the Sex Pistols.

"Dude! I'm totally serious! You're Tim frickin' Dorsey!"

At this point, Tim stopped walking. He wasn't saying anything, but I'm pretty sure he was contemplating his fight-or-flight options.

"Huge fan!" I shouted. "Huge fan. Huge frickin' fan. Dude, you're awesome! Love your stuff! Where do you come up with it? Huge frickin' fan! Let me buy you a beer!"

"Hey, normally, count me in," he said, "but I'm, uh, thinking through a column and I'm headed home."

"Awesome! We can drink beer at your house!"

As you can imagine, Tim was giving me a very strange look. I didn't know what to do—he was Tim (frickin') Dorsey, and if there was one fact I knew, it was that we *were* going to drink a beer together. Then, it struck me. I knew exactly what to say.

"Dude, I'm not, like, a psycho—just a fan!"

Tim's look got even weirder.

"Come on, dude! One beer!"

My next cogent memory has me and Tim climbing out the window onto the roof of the three-story house where he and ten other guys lived. I don't know why the roof had such appeal, but who was I to complain? Who among us doesn't enjoy roof drinking? One beer turned into six, and we discussed majoring in journalism versus English, my decision to go into the Marine Corps and his decision to be a newspaperman, and at some point, I recall telling him about my recent near-DUI on my K-Mart bicycle. I also remember telling Tim he was way too talented to write for a mere newspaper.

Fade. To. Black.

Twenty Years Later

I was in a bookstore in Charleston, South Carolina, looking to see if they had any more books from one of my new, favorite authors—some unknown guy named Tim Dorsey. His books centered around the adventures of a lovable psychopath named Serge A. Storms and his stoner buddy Coleman, and easily qualified as some of the funniest books I'd ever read.

I looked through the paperback section and found nothing new, and was on my way out when I saw a hardcover titled *Hurricane Punch* by none other than Tim Dorsey. I picked it up, flipped to the inside back of the dustcover, and discovered a little bio information: Wow, this dude went to *Auburn*. I knew a guy who went to Auburn named Tim Dorsey, didn't I? This Tim Dorsey was a former reporter for the Tampa newspaper. Didn't the Tim Dorsey I knew plan to be a journalist? Tim Dorsey … Tim Dorsey … Tim Dor— Holy crap! This guy was Tim (frickin') Dorsey!

Back at home, I googled Tim and found his website—and it was then that I realized how big-time he'd gotten. He had an e-store full of Serge Storms merchandise, several other books out. Hell, he was a famous author and everything. I decided to email his site, in hopes that he might remember me:

Tim, I doubt you'll remember me, but we met one night at Auburn when I was on the way home from a Tri Delt party.

We ended up on the roof of your house, and I drank so many of your beers, I almost fell to an untimely end. If you have any recollection of that fateful night, shoot me an email!

Three days later came a reply:

You mean the night you told me you almost got arrested for drunken biking? Wearing a cape? THAT night?

I promptly placed an order directly through Tim for a hardback version of every one of his books. I would have liked to stay in touch, but—hey, the dude is famous. He's a successful author. I figured that if I pursued a friendship, I'd end up asking him to read a manuscript … and I just couldn't do it to him.

Current Day

I'd emailed Tim about once a year, just to let him know that I'd read his latest book, or seen an article on him, or had encountered a big Tim Dorsey display in some faraway airport. I asked him once about struggling author stuff, and he responded that struggling was the life of a published author, too—and not to quit my day job.

Then, one day, I was feeling overwhelmed by my cluelessness—I'd been on a book tour and still didn't know what the hell was going on. Given that there's not exactly a community of published authors down at the local bar you bitch with, I emailed Tim:

Dude,

You TOTALLY failed to tell me about signings/ events for first-time authors.

I was in Chicago for an event on Tuesday, and the manager had the wrong date posted.

I gave my dog & pony show to three people in Palm Beach.

In Westland, a crowd of 20 showed up, and I had them all rolling in the aisles, then took about 15 questions … and sold zero books.

Do you still drink? I do.

Throw me a frickin' bone here, man. Any wise-old-successful-writer-man nuggets are appreciated.

War Eagle,
Prioleau

Hey, Man. It's Tim Dorsey

A week later, Tim called. Here, at last, was a battle-hardened veteran who could provide me with the answers I so desired. With ten books under his belt and the most recent one on the *New York Times* bestseller list, I just *knew* he could pull me aboard his vessel, issue me my own lifeboat, and set me sailing toward the shores of success and fame, guided by fair winds and following seas. What would his first words be? What choice motivational nuggets would he offer that would give me the encouragement to stay afloat?

"Welcome to hell," he said.

We talked for about thirty minutes, and Tim told me that my trials and tribulations were the same ones experienced by every first-time author. Concerning his first book tour, he stated flatly that he felt "like someone in the witness protection program."

With Tim on the phone, I ran through some of my remaining questions about the business I wanted to ask him. Let's see: Will I make any money? Can't ask that. When do I get to find out how my book is selling? Can't ask that. How long before I should submit my next manuscript? Dumb question. Wait! I have a question I can ask!

"Any promotional advice? Ideas that worked for you?"

"Here's the deal," he said. "Most writers who get lucky enough to be published are two-and-out, and that's even if you sign with a big publishing house. If you want to make writing your *career*, you've got to suck it up, knock on doors, promote yourself and your book, and do all the stuff that's the exact opposite of your nature as a writer."

"Bringing back fond memories, eh?" I asked.

"I'll never forget," Tim replied, then told me a story:

> After my very first book got published, I stopped by a big-box bookstore to introduce

myself to the manager and give her a signed copy of my book—you know, make a good impression, schmooze a little. So, I tracked down the information desk and asked the lady there if I could speak to the manager.

The lady asks, "And you are?"

I tell her I'm Tim Dorsey—a new author—and my first book has just shipped. I just want to introduce myself to the manager and tell her a little about the book.

She disappears for a few minutes, and comes back. "I'm sorry," she says, "but the manager is unavailable to meet with you right now."

No problem, I figure. *It's lunchtime, and she probably wants to enjoy her sandwich in peace.*

So I tell the lady, "Look, I don't have to be anywhere. I'll go grab some coffee in the café, and read a book until she gets back from lunch."

"Oh, she's not at lunch," the lady says. "She's in the children's section fixing a shelf."

I had a few more laughs with Tim, and before long, we rang off. But I will confess to feeling a little conflicted. I felt *encouraged* by Tim, as he had "sucked it up for a bit" and his labors had resulted in his fantastic successes. But the sad truth in my case, I feared, was that the flame required to act on his advice had burned out with my career in advertising. I thought writing was a career that would allow me to disappear into the shadows, and the truth was emerging as something very different.

THE BIG IDEA EMERGES

What Are the Odds?

I don't think anyone realizes how many books are published until they have their own little book out there in the pond, struggling for air, panicked, eager to grab hold of anything offering buoyancy—even if it means latching onto a grandmother holding her grandchild. *Pre*publication, you enter a bookstore unknowingly fitted with "intellectual blinders" that keep you from actually seeing those thousands of titles; it's an instinctual defense mechanism, lest the depth of what you *don't* know—on hundreds of subjects—cause your frontal lobe to implode.

Post-publication, however, you see them all ... and every book in a bookstore takes on the face of the enemy, poised as both seductress and highwayman, ready to intercept any buyers who might be wandering in the direction of your book.

Even the experience of innocently *entering* a bookstore changes once your first published book hits the shelves. What was once an exciting experience *(What new books will I discover?)* becomes, well, an embarrassing experience *(What if someone who knows me sees me and thinks I'm here lurking and hard-selling my book to lonely souls wandering toward the self-help section?)*. Like Billy Pilgrim in Vonnegut's zoo, for me, entering a bookstore began to feel like entering a display case, where curious onlookers could watch and wonder about my single-dimensional view of my surroundings—a place where I was no longer able to experience the holistic joy of shared ideas, but was doomed to peer down the six-foot peephole at my book alone, wondering if, in fact, "That's life."

Field Trip

Thinking about the bookstore has inspired a field trip to my town's Barnes and Noble bookstore, because part of the store is a coffeehouse. The venture is based on my reading about all the successful writers who claim to have written their first book in a coffeehouse, not the least of whom is British writer J. K. Rowling, who is richer than most of the grifters in the Royal Family.

Coffeeshops and places like them must be inspiring and motivational, because on the very rare occasions when I've splurged on burnt, overbrewed coffee myself, it seems the joint is brimming with people hammering away on their laptops. Are these great writers writing great books? Maybe. Today will perhaps tell the tale.

This outing feels right to me—at the very least, I can drink coffee, write a little, and hard-sell my book to people on the way to the self-help section. But what should I wear? The phrase "What should I wear?" has never passed through my mind before, but suddenly, this seems important. Surely black is the correct color, but the only black items I own are my funeral suit and a USMC T-shirt that says, "Don't bother running. You'll just die tired."

Maybe a bohemian look? Or is bohemian a smell? I don't have any tie-dye … no crunchy T-shirts lamenting the lack of Air Force bake sales … no retro plaid trousers or tight silk shirts. Oh, well. Guess I'll just have to hearken back to the words of my dear old grandmother: Screw it.

One Small Step for Man

I'm in the bookstore/coffeeshop. The first thing that lands in my field of vision is a sign stating that the café section is for paying customers only, so I make my move to the counter. It is vital to avoid drawing attention to myself. *(Attention, security—we have a one-book author loitering in the café, trying to look aloof and superior and pathetically hoping one of his readers will recognize him, which isn't mathematically possible unless his mom or his wife walks in.*

Security, please respond. Code Taser.) I make eye contact with the girl at the counter.

ME: Do you have iced coffee?

GAL: You bet. What would you like?

ME: I was down in Florida with a buddy and he turned me on to this really tasty iced coffee. Do they come in flavors?

GAL: Sure: vanilla, hazelnut, chocolate, caramel, strawberry—

ME: You have strawberry coffee?

GAL: Oh, yes. It's yummy.

ME: Sounds weird. Like salsa ice cream.

GAL: Lots of people love it.

ME: I think I'd like caramel iced coffee, please. Large.

GAL: Very good. One vinti frappa-schwappa-latte-half-caf-de-caf-no-foam-ice, coming up. Hey, I see you have your laptop. You going to do some writing?

ME: No! I mean, what makes you think that?

GAL: It's what some people do when they bring a laptop with them.

ME: God, no. I'm gonna use the wireless internet.

GAL: We've certainly got that.

Me: So, uh, thanks. I'll be over here doing a little web surfing. Maybe some research on bear hunting naked, armed only with a knife.

Gal: Okay.

Me: Maybe bomb defusing, too …

Feel the Flow

I'm looking around. To my left there's a large guy, writing. He's kind of got the Nelson DeMille thing going on. I suspect he's writing a thriller based in Berzerkestan with CIA operatives named Colt Unitas and Russian KGB guys with names like Khrzxstlmsnbg Zxgrhxztr. But maybe not.

Across from me are some kids. To my right is a yummy mummy, reading an *Elle* magazine with an intensity normally reserved for politicians looking for loopholes in ethics laws. I ponder the women's magazine phenomenon for a bit. How many are there? How many are sold every month? How many billions of dollars change hands? How many recipes can be developed?

Pondering the topic of women's magazines, my mind wanders to the primary topics they explore. Of course, there's the critical need to know which stars are now too fat, which are too skinny, and which are getting repeat-customer discounts at rehab. I also wonder about the never-ending cover story promising a pathway to multiple orgasms. With well over forty-five women's magazines on the shelves of this bookstore alone, and all those magazines coming out with the same orgasmic promise every month … that's 45 times 12, which equals 540 multiple orgasm *solutions* a year. Multiply that by five years, and—hell, I'm surprised they aren't writing about ways to *avoid* multiple orgasms at this point. How can you get anything done?

But.

But … am I really different from the writers for *Elle* magazine? If so, can I really point to how we are different?

Yes. Yes, I can. Their writing is read by hundreds of thousands of people, while mine is read by, well, less. A lot less. They are writing to the largest reading and book-buying demographic in America (women), and I write to a smaller group (me, my publisher, and the people I promise to mention by name in the acknowledgments). They cover topics that they know, for a fact, people are interested in, and I serial-type for months at a time on topics that refuse to leave me alone. Quite simply, I *have* to write. But I sure as hell wouldn't mind a few hundred thousand people buying my book.

But how does one generate sales? What do I know, for a fact, that readers actually want to read about? Recipes, obviously. Celebrity gossip. Clearly, multiple orgasms are extremely popular. And to attract a few male readers, it's important to remember the thriller and mystery genre.

Aha! It's so clear now! The key is to expand *past* my target audience and reach out to the book-buying public at large. And based on what I can tell, the *title* of the book is a hell of a lot more important than the content.

This visit to the bookstore may have inspired the perfect book title. Just listen to the flow:

The Hollywood Stars' Cookbook to Lose Weight with No Effort, and Enjoy Multiple Orgasms— Uncover the Mystery of It All!

Digging deeper, I discover that in this bookstore alone, there are 57 placards designating *genres* of books. Under the genre *For Dog Lovers*, there are 21 titles. How the hell do you get traction with all that competition? How do you break through the clutter and get buyers to at least *pick up* your book? Hell—you simply use the *title* to mark your bookstore territory like a two-year-old Lab at a doggie park!

The right title will enable my new book to rest comfortably in multiple locations throughout the bookstore. I just need to make sure my new concept covers all the genres. Does my new concept successfully accomplish that?

Cookbooks: Obviously covered.

Relationships: Covered.

Self-Improvement: Based on the promises of my cover, you'll soon forget about all the little issues troubling you!

Science Fiction: At least *some* gals must consider the concept of multiple orgasms sci-fi, or they wouldn't keep buying the magazines searching for the source, right?

Mystery: See above.

Fantasy: Combine cooking, orgasms, Hollywood gossip, and maybe a glass or two of wine? Are you kidding me? Put Megan Fox and her machine-gunner boyfriend on the cover, and they'd have to issue a new currency for my quarterly royalties: the gazillion-dollar bill.

Romance: Once the word of this title leaks out, sales to men within the romance genre will *dwarf* crime and mystery.

Crafts: Housebound on a rainy day? My title sounds like it offers a hell of a new hobby.

True Crime: I'm thinking there will be more than a murder or two of insensitive men who forget to have this title wrapped and under the Christmas tree.

Literature: After the title tricks enough people into buying enough copies, I'm thinking it will have to be accepted as a de facto classic. Ever finished *Anna Karenina*? Me neither, but it's in a ton of libraries.

Investing: The ability to deliver multiple orgasms to their partner would be considered a very wise investment of time and money by even the nerdiest of men.

Humor: Won't everyone think it's funny when they find the main title is complete bull crap?

Puzzles: See above, under Sci-Fi and Mystery.

Travel: See Fantasy. No one will ever want to leave their house again!

This could be the secret! The way I bust through! If I can get noticed as this mega-hit author, I can then transition into writing what I actually *want* to write, and act all mysterious and conflicted and deep.

"I feel," I'll say to the *New Yorker*, "as though my exploration of cookbooks and orgasms has reached its creative conclusion, and now I will be exploring new ways to spread my wings as a writer and thinker."

With that, I'll switch over to humorous nonfiction, and attack anyone who challenges me for being a creative-phobic.

"How dare you challenge my decision to pass on a sequel to the orgasmic cookbook! Did Fitzgerald write *Gatsby II?* Yes, I know he couldn't because Gatsby was dead—but I'm making a point, fool! Thinkers like I cannot simply ignore the song-lines that guide our journey! The heart cries out to explore, and explore I must!"

I ponder this idea with laser focus, and conclude it ranks up there with my idea for a dot-com company selling fresh fish via snail mail.

I put the idea in my rearview mirror.

PLEASE ... SHUT UP

Blogs? Again?

As I treaded water there in the Great Lake of Self-Doubt, the idea of emailing my editor to ask for advice bubbled to the surface. I'd been feeling a little blue because the "fan" email coming into my website had been silent for a couple of weeks straight. Fan mail is an exterior validation; it proves you not only wooed your publisher, but also managed to impress a few readers who didn't already know you. I'd never much experienced that before. Praise for my writing in the past had come in the form of a check, payable to the ad agency I worked for. That was pretty much it.

"You're doing great," my editor wrote back, and it occurred to me that those are the exact same words people use to encourage tubby kids playing kickball. "Maybe you could do some research on blogs, and see if you can drum up some interest from them."

"I'm on it … *to the tilt!*" It sounded like a nice way to try to stay warm while my spirits plummeted faster than Jack's body temperature, floating in the North Sea and wishing Rose would make a little more room atop that door. …

Always Happy to Hear from You!

Once again, my brain decided it was time to stop in for a chat.

VOICE: How things going?

ME: Not so good. I'm doing lots of second-guessing about this dream of being a successful writer.

VOICE: Well, hell—I've been trying to get you to dump that stupid idea for twenty years. You remember? You were a lieutenant on Okinawa, sitting in your officer's quarters, writing your manuscript about the trials and tribulations of turning thirty. I told you right then and there you were wasting your time.

ME: Well, I made it, didn't I? I got published.

VOICE: Yup. Reached your dream. Now you're drunk on a tiny bit of recognition, and you've been dreaming of ways to get stuff published you don't even want to write. You write nonfiction humor, so write nonfiction humor! You hit the grand slam and actually got one of your works published—and now you're ready to sell out already? Why the hell do you write?

ME: Because I can't *not* write.

VOICE: So you're thinking about orgasmic cookbooks just to get your next book published? You don't deserve to call yourself a writer.

ME: I think you're right.

VOICE: Write about what you love writing about. The public may never read it, but your grandkids will, once they realize Pop-Pop has a manuscript in the attic. That's more than good enough, you yo-yo. You'll live on through your work—even if you don't make a dime.

ME: I know … it's different than I expected.

VOICE: Huh. You mean it didn't somehow fulfill your every need? Gee, what a shocker. What's your beef now?

ME: Sometimes I just feel despair. I mean, will my next book get published? Will getting a second book published feel more fulfilling?

VOICE: Let's talk expectations. What do you need to get out of life to achieve happiness?

ME: As a Christian?

VOICE: Let's leave your religion out of this. As a regular schmoe, what is it you want your writing to achieve?

ME: First, financial security.

VOICE: Okay, forget that. If you need that, you'd better get a job with the government.

ME: Then I guess hoping for financial luxuries wouldn't be a good second choice.

VOICE: We're talking about what you *need*, not what you want.

ME: I guess the same thing every artist wants: validation. For people to read my books and learn something, or reflect on something, or at least have a short mental vacation from the worries of the world.

VOICE: Did you achieve that with the first book?

ME: Among the people who read it, I think so ... I just don't know how many people read it. It's sold about sixteen thousand copies. I'm told that's an insane amount for a first-time author. It was either dumb luck, endless marketing on my part, or maybe some people actually liked it.

VOICE: So that's the problem, right? That's what has you feeling despair?

ME: Yeah. The result of achieving a dream is supposed to be bigger, isn't it? Shouldn't it be like the feeling of reaching the summit of Everest? Standing atop the mountain—so high up, you need oxygen—and reveling in the accomplishment.

VOICE: So you think most mountain climbers who summit Everest retire? They climbed the big one, so now it's off to the rocking chair? Their call of the wild gets left up there with their footprints and sweat?

Me: I'd think they—you know, at least revel a bit.

Voice: So how long *should* they stand there and revel?

Me: I don't know. No one ever explains that part of the dream.

Voice: Well, aren't there other people climbing that very same mountain? Don't you have to make room for them, too? Before long, don't you have to get out of the way, so the follow-on climbers can stand on the summit?

Me: You could fight to keep your spot there.

Voice: Oh, that sounds pleasant. You mean, like an aging Hollywood starlet spending six months every year getting plastic surgery? Or a television has-been agreeing to be on a reality show?

Me: So, what's the answer?

Voice: Hey, you're the one who latched onto the weird, subjective, never-quite-there dream. How many people would announce plans to climb Everest if there were no summit? When your dream is to climb a mountain, you strive to reach the summit. When your dream is to graduate college, you strive to get your diploma. But you—you and all the other crazy writers out there—y'all have chosen a very, very different path. Y'all are climbing a mountain without a top. My advice is for you to dream of finishing *this* manuscript, and reworking it, and pushing yourself until you say, "I did it. *That's my summit.* If the rest of the world never sees it, that's their loss. At least the world will be a better place for the rare individuals who do actually see my work."

ME: That's … that's actually good advice. You never give good advice. You just bitch at me. I'm really appreciative.

VOICE: Go get some sun, man. You look unhealthy.

The Full-time Writing Gig

I am currently able to write part-time for one reason, and one reason only: my wife. We don't have kids, and she believes I have "the stuff" to one day be discovered in a financially viable way, so together we live a pretty simple life, supported by her work at our church and my sporadic consulting jobs.

This is a new thing for me—remember, I wrote my first three manuscripts, one of which died just before crossing the finish line, when I was working fifty or sixty hours a week. Given this gift of time and space, I think about all the incredible, history-making writers who've taken the full-time dare, and I am awed to find myself even attempting to walk their trail. The experience is exciting, frightening, thrilling. I ponder and write and search for clues that I'm on the right path. How can one know?

The most romantic of all full-time writing groups, of course, is the Lost Generation of the 1920s—a group of ex-pat writers, artists, and poets in post–World War I Paris. Disillusioned by the war and having watched their very moral code destroyed by cannon fire and the horror of trench warfare, this group of famed artisans spent much of the decade drinking, conversing, and challenging the norms of the world as they knew it. Not fighting, of course—the only one who ever heard a shot fired in anger was Hemingway. The Lost Generation didn't actually do much but lay the groundwork for future hippies, except with fewer drug options, better clothes, and the ability to write sentences longer than "Arms Are for Hugging."

The "get back to work" ethic of America after World War I seemed hollow and pointless, and together, the Lost Generation rewrote the rules of literature, poetry, and what constituted acceptable blood alcohol content. The names of the writers associated with the Lost Generation read like a classics section of American literature: T. S. Eliot, Ezra Pound, Gertrude Stein, Ernest Hemingway, F. Scott and Zelda Fitzgerald, Sherwood Anderson, Ford Maddox Ford … one can only imagine the hilarity of these self-important poofters staggering around the Left Bank, and passing out under the urinal at the Dingo Bar.

Consider the endurance required to hang around these people: espresso with Eliot, hearing his plans to freak out English professors; lunch with Hemingway, where he punches you in the face for telling him you think he's trying to compensate for something; a dozen drinks with Scott and Zelda, and you wondering if you're going to have to kill one of the great writers in American history if his wife doesn't shut up; finally, a dinner party until two in the morning with the whole gang over at rue de Fleurus. Even contemplating the day is exhausting—the haze of French cigarettes, spilled red wine on linen, roaring arguments about who will be remembered as the greatest writer; after a long weekend, I'd be signing up for trench warfare.

As a writer, I cannot help but wonder if I am experiencing the same level of social intercourse as these early geniuses—forced to defend my beliefs and opinions against minds honed by the whetting stone of disillusionment. As an exercise, one day I monitored every word I said aloud every time I took a break from writing. Here's a look:

Who wants some breakfast? Are we hungry? Is it time? Is it time already? So soon? That's my good girls. Good girls! I see you! I see you! I see those tails wagging!

Twenty minutes later.

Who needs to go out? Who needs to go out? Who needs to go out?

Three hours later.

Who wants to go for a walk? Yes? Yes? That's my good girls!

You get the picture.

I might need to go back to working full-time.

Good Friend; Bad Idea

One day, I planned to have lunch with my closest friend, John. A Renaissance Man in every sense of the word (as it applies to locations south of DC, north of Jacksonville, and east of New Orleans), John had played a fairly-significant-yet-anonymous role in my earlier book, and he can be counted on to challenge my current beliefs on just about any topic, save religion.

He is a medical doctor able to fix your sputtering diesel engine; he is a loving father able to build your next home; he is a generous friend who can, with no formal training, also fly your airplane safely from Point A to Point B. And to top it off, he is one of only two people I know who has performed in an internationally acclaimed opera. He seemed like just the guy for me to engage in some thought-provoking banter, and reconnect with the challenges of introspection. Above all else, John was a realist, and wouldn't suffer my whining gladly. I needed some practical advice regarding my path forward.

We chose as our luncheon spot a Greek restaurant, and placed our order for gyros, cucumber salads, and iced tea. It was cool for a July afternoon in Charleston, and we sat outside and watched as the pelicans made their way inland from a morning on the creek. The spot was a bit more strip-mall-ish than Left-Bank-ish, but *c'est la vie*.

ME: You know, I've been thinking, I need to find something to do professionally—in addition to writing. The manuscript is coming along nicely, but I gotta make some money. The checkbook is emptier than Joe Biden's brain. Heidi suggested that if I wasn't going to make any money, maybe I could pitch in by washing and reusing our doggie-poo bags.

JOHN: Be an activist.

ME: How do you become an activist?

JOHN: It's easy. You just form a nonprofit and make yourself the CEO. Nonprofit CEOs are making a hundred-fifty these days.

ME: What's the cause?

JOHN: The cause?

ME: Yeah. What's the cause I'm being an activist about?

JOHN: Well, you're in it for the money, so here's an idea: Start a charity to cheer on the underdog billionaires.

ME: Billionaires are underdogs?

JOHN: No, but they're stinkin' rich. Start a website called billionaires-making-a-difference.com. Write up a bunch of obsequious crap about how great the Facebook guy and Warren Buffett and Jeff Bezos are for giving away money. Make up stories about Elon flying commercial because he loaned his jet to fly a manatee to a Jimmy Buffett concert. You kidding me?

Someone saying nice stuff about them? Those fat cats will be sponsoring your website so fast, you'll need a cash-counting machine.

ME: There is the slight problem—those dicks don't give away enough for it really matter. If you're worth eighty billion, and dole out a billion to your own foundation—that you control—that gets pretty transparent pretty quick.

JOHN: No problem—lie.

ME: How do you lie about giving billions of dollars?

JOHN: Dude, even the head of the IRS doesn't understand these oligarchs' money-hiding schemes. No one knows what's where—ever. Tell the media four billion was given through Mr. Bezos's sub-C Corp "Blessings to Others," which is a foundation controlled by Make Me Look Good, LLC, a wholly-owned subsidiary of I Love Me, Inc. Tell them it's incorporated in Afghanistan. You're dealing with journalism majors. As long as they don't claim the donation on their taxes, no harm, no foul.

ME: So ... sell out? That's the short of it? Use a gift God gave me to make some of the most awful men in the world look good?

JOHN: You want to get away from the sellout system? I hear the Amish are accepting converts.

And thus, with my wits re-honed to a razor's edge, I returned home. To greet me at the door were two good girls, whom I asked, "Who wants Daddy to make Mark Zuckerberg look noble? Tell everyone George Soros is a hero?"

Maddie bit me.

Let the Sun Shine

I decided that if I was going to take the advice of the Voice and get some sun, I needed to find my way out of the shade of ignorance where I was currently living. There were still some questions I needed answered, despite the fact that almost a year had passed since being told my book would be published, and four months since the day the book shipped. My agent had never been one for answering the kinds of sensitive questions I always had in my head, probably because he knew I wouldn't really want to know the honest answers. But, in the words of that prone street punk in the film *Dirty Harry*: "*I gots to know!*" Odds are, if you're reading this, you're likely a fellow writer, so once again, I remind you—ask the questions I didn't:

1. How is my book selling, all things considered?
2. Is there anything I can do to coddle, tempt, or beg book reviewers for big newspapers to review my book, or is my four-month-old book now ancient history?

3. Does it look like I will make more money than my advance, or is the advance pretty much the sum total of my income?
4. Is there some sort of secret publishing-industry blacklist I'm now on, and categorized as "has trouble focusing during class"?
5. What should I be aware of prior to making my next submission?
6. Is there anything I can do to woo the big-box booksellers?

Stones Left Unturned

It occurred to me that there was still a stone left unturned in my quest for answers. Actually, there were two: First, there was my contact at my publisher—a hell of a nice guy—but I still didn't really understand the relationship between the author and the publisher. But there was also the guy known as the "sales rep," Michael. I'd been CCed on a couple of emails to him, and I knew he was the guy out there on the road who'd been pitching my book to actual bookstores. I could clearly recall the first time I heard about the "sales rep" from my agent:

AGENT: The publisher tells me the sales rep really likes your book.

ME: That's good?

AGENT: It's huge. It's like having the ultimate book review.

ME: How so? I don't even know what a sales rep does.

AGENT: He's the guy who calls on stores and tells them what books are coming on the market. He's got a huge binder with page after page of books, and each book cover is about the size of a postage stamp. For him to point at *your* postage stamp and say, "This one is good" is about as big a break as a rookie could hope for.

I was thrilled … and (as usual) depressed. My sweet, innocent, lovely little baby book arrived into the world as but a mere postage stamp among hundreds. How could this be? I realize, of course, this postage-stamp-size promo is something every unpublished author would love to have—but if I've said it once, I'll say it again: I was a rookie idiot. I don't blame readers for laughing at my dumbassedry, but hey—did you know about the postage-stamp thing?

Anyway, I had something a little more in-depth in mind than said postage stamp—you know, a group of bookstore owners wining and dining me, all gathered around a vast round table at Elaine's, each having been flown in by the publisher. After a sumptuous meal and many, many bottles of very fine wine, the sales rep would announce, "Well, ladies and gentlemen … the moment we've all been waiting for. We'll start on my left, and go around the table, and each of you will announce *your* favorite part of Prioleau Alexander's breakthrough work of nonfiction."

And so on.

I decided to email the sales rep and ask him if he would be willing to answer some of my questions. Bless him, he said yes—and we set up a time to talk on the phone. Here's what I learned:

1. How is my book selling? *Classified information —it involves the issue of royalty payments, so it can only be discussed by the publisher.*

2. Is there anything I can do to coddle, tempt, or beg book reviewers for big newspapers? *That would be nice but, oops—most newspapers have fired their book reviewers. The ones who do review books mostly only review titles by the monstrous-sized publishers who might run an ad.*

3. Does it look like I will make more money than my advance? *See number one, above.*

4. What should I be aware of prior to making my next submission? *What the hell do I know? I'm in sales.*

5. Is there anything I can do to woo the big-box booksellers? *Yes—just as soon as you have people waiting in line at midnight to buy your next book.*

The most valuable information centered on Michael's advice from his years on the road. If you are a writer, this is stuff you need to know. It'll give you a semi-bitter taste of reality, but it can help you understand what's demanded of you—whether you sell your book to a monster publisher or a small house:

- As discussed earlier, publishing is a business, and a business exists to earn profits. The publisher takes a big financial gamble with every new author just by editing, designing, and printing the books. It's the author's job to help sell books, so the publisher can make back that gambled money. At the end of the day, the business is about making profits, not discovering new talent.

- Just as the publisher's loyalty must be to their business, your loyalty, as the author, must be to your book. The publisher will promote it in every cost-efficient way they can, but it won't be as much as you (or any writer) would want. If you hope to take your book to higher places, *you've* got to take it to higher places. Maybe one in twenty thousand writers gets to become a traditionally published author. Only a handful of authors will reach the point of commercial success without personally busting their ass doing promotion, marketing, and sales.

- Employees in bookstores sell books. If you take the time to drive to their store to meet them, shake their hand, and tell them about yourself, they will be interested in you. If your book is good, they will recommend it to buyers. It's human nature: People care more about people who care about them. This is why big publishers spend the money to send authors on a book tour. If you go with a small outfit or decide to self-publish, all the book marketing falls a hundred percent on you, and you alone.

- If the publisher's investment in promoting your book is enough for you, great. If you dream of seeing your book break out and achieve great things, you need to get to work.

A Walk of Reflection

Having taken that exhaustive step of generating actual business, and with not much else happening in my writing life, I thought it would be the perfect time to refocus on writing the book you're reading now. Some magazine reported that author Charles Frazier used to go for long walks in the mountains while writing his opus *Cold Mountain*, to reflect and actually see the things his protagonist would have seen while walking home from the war. Considering Charles Frazier sold a gazillion copies of *Cold Mountain*, I decided this might be a good exercise for me to try. My wife and I live out in the country, so surely the countryside would offer me the same creative muse that it provided Mr. Frazier.

I left the driveway and began my wanderings along the dirt road that leads to our home. I had just begun to marvel at all the wonders of the natural world, when a fairly sizable rock worked its way between my heel and my left Teva. My back was bothering me a bit, and I knew sitting down to dislodge the interloper would no doubt prove painful. Then, it hit me: I could use my right foot to bend back the rubber heel of the left sandal, then let it go. The flicking action would shoot the rock out, and allow me to continue my quest for enlightenment without so much as a brief stutter-step.

What happened next defied all laws of probability, and proved beyond a shadow of a doubt that chaos theory is more law than theory. When I flicked the rock, it proceeded directly upward at near-warp speed, managed to thread its way through the gap between my boxers and my leg, and impacted my family stones with laser-guided precision.

The pain literally dropped me to my knees, bad back and everything. As I knelt there, stunned and gasping, all thoughts of enlightenment and nature and beauty and inspiration vaporized. All I could think was, "I've kicked myself in the nads. How can anyone kick themselves in the nads?" It occurred to me as I wobbled back up my driveway that perhaps, just perhaps, I had discovered something new under the sun.

Maybe I should write a book about "new things under the sun"?

OUCH, MY HEAD

Who Built This Ceiling I Keep Hitting My Head on?

A few years back, Kevin Costner starred in wonderful golf movie entitled *Tin Cup*, about a driving-range pro who enters the U.S. Open and plays brilliantly. At one point, he is making a run at the course record, when one of the television producers laments that so much of the attention of the broadcast is being stolen by a "nobody"—a mere driving-range pro held the viewing audience in the palm of his hand, and the usual big-shot pros were getting ignored: "It's heroes I need," he rants, "not obscure driving-range pros."

Indeed.

America loves champions—the more dominant and longer-reigning, the better. Whether it's athletes, actors, musicians, or writers, we want our American gods placed up high. Out of reach. Invincible. Yet humble. Wise. Knowing. Deserving. We want them up there, on the throne, until *their* desire to reign slips past—at which point they should step down, undefeated, only then making way for a new, equally invincible champion. *Of course,* there are pockets of aficionados in every area—fans who truly understand and study the nuances and subtleties of their area of interest—but in general? The fact is that most Americans want the driving-range pros to *stay* on the driving range … much like they want new writers to stop taking up space on the bookstore shelves.

Why?

Could it be because *invincible* champions are safely beyond the scope of our own dreams? And challengers remind us of who we really are: mere scrappers, fighting for ten-thousandth place? If every "champion" were a one-hit/fight/game/match/tournament wonder, then what would that say about me? You see, a revolving door of champions would remind us daily that we never even made it into the arena. But a long-reigning champion? It feels right. Distant. Unattainable. Superhuman. You can't feel inferior to super-mega-monster-level greatness: the Rolling Stones. Muhammad Ali. Michael Crichton. JFK. Bo Jackson. John Elway. Yo-Yo Ma. Pavarotti. Tiger Woods. It is *stars* we love, not for the light they provide, but for the light years they are away from us.

Did You and I Co-build This Damn Ceiling?

When you go into a bookstore, who do you ask about—your usual favorite authors? Or do you ask if there are any rookie authors in the store—authors breaking the usual rules and exploring new ideas?

Reading is a serious time commitment, and when I carve out the time for it, it's a slam dunk I'm seeking—something I *know* will be good. And for good or ill, there are lots of great established authors I know will entertain me.

So the question is this: Do you and I support ... *you and I?* Or do we purchase books written by authors who don't need our support? I, for one, have searched out new and emerging authors working in my favorite genres, and it pains me to say it, but they just didn't have the chops that some of the big names do. It's one-hundred-percent possible they will one day, given the time to mature as writers, but they need our support *now*.

And there's only one way those rookie authors are going to get my support: by marketing to me, convincing me they deserve a shot, offering damn fine work, and asking me to take a chance and buy their book. Buying me a few martinis at Happy Hour wouldn't, you know, hurt ... but when you're buying every potential book buyer martinis, either your liver or your wallet is gonna collapse before your next submission.

That's the only way unknown writers like you and I are going to break through. It ain't fair, but neither is the fact James Patterson no longer even bothers to write his own books.

Aaaaand ... Action!

I quit thinking, and got to work ... the time came to stop grumbling, heed that sales rep's advice, and get out there and fearlessly promote my book. On the road. Lock horns with the bookstore owners, and sell them on carrying my book. No point in whining when there's work to be done. I had several business and personal trips planned to southeastern cities that weren't on the book tour my publisher had arranged, so during the next month, I brought a case of books with me on my travels. From there, it was simply a matter of knocking on bookstore doors—I was Willy Loman in his prime, busting through doors with a shoeshine and a smile, brimming with pluck and cheer.

Whether a store was indie or big-box, I tracked down the owner or manager and did the soft-shoe. Sure, there was lots of standing in line while the manager assisted little old ladies seeking "that book, by that guy, about that thing," but I was as patient as old Screwtape himself, awaiting my moment to pounce.

It was an interesting exercise. Though most of the indie owners I called on were absolutely delightful, I did run into a few who offered a less-than-chipper response. I made notes, as sometimes the exchange was too incredible to believe.

Picture me standing in front of this bookstore owner, hat in my hand, having just told them about the amazing reviews on Amazon, the jobs I'd worked, and the blurbs I'd received from some huge names. The dialogue below is exactly as it happened—not one word is added for comedic value.

Action!

ME: … So, I thought I'd personally bring by a review copy of my book. I've learned that the people who sell books are people in bookstores, so I'm comin' to the source!

OWNER: I guess I could put it on my stack of stuff to read.

ME: I really think you'll like it—Pat Conroy gave it a great review!

OWNER: Pat Conroy will give a blurb to anybody.

Aaaaaand … cut!

ME: … so I'm comin' to the source!

OWNER: Great. I'll read it.

ME: Cool. Would you like me to sign it?

OWNER: Sure.

ME: Tell me your name so I can personalize it.

OWNER: Nah, just sign it. If you put my name on it, I can't sell it.

Aaaaaand ... cut!

ME: ... so I'm comin' to the source!

OWNER: What a lousy time to be a writer. Three hundred thousand books were released last year. Self-publishing is up, and readership is down.

Aaaaaand ... cut!

ME: ... to the source!

OWNER: Are these books returnable?

Aaaaaaand ... cut!

ME: ... so, you know, I just drive around with a box of these freakin' boat anchors in my car, and—hell, I'll *give* you one if you'll just lie to me and say you'll read it.

OWNER: I did read it. A friend gave me their copy. I loved it.

ME: Okay, thanks anyway. Bye.

This going-to-the-source thing wasn't working out exactly as I planned. Idealism was morphing into wisdom, then oozing downhill into a bucket of fatalism, which was overflowing and spilling onto a cup of ugly realism.

It was a cup from which I had no desire to drink ... but I added some good tequila, a lime, and some salt, and it went down easier.

THE RULES OF COMBAT

As the executive officer of a company while in the Marines, I had three rules of combat posted on my wall:

1. Perfect plans aren't.
2. When in doubt, flip to full auto and empty the magazine.
3. It's easier to be resupplied with bullets than opportunities.

One of my lieutenants, a close friend, made a good point after reading those rules for the thousandth time.

"That's too much crap for my boys to remember," he said. "As my wise and insightful XO, I need you to sum them up. Something pithy, yet useful."

In response, I replaced them:

1. Attack.
2. Attack.
3. Attack.

That pretty much sums up why the Marines are so successful, and why Americans love their Marine Corps. Marines attack—always. Of all the armed forces, they have the fewest men, the worst gear, the fewest resources, and (usually) the most hazardous mission ... but despite it all, they attack.

The Army, Navy, and Air Force might have better technology, but Americans love the Marines because Marines take the most real estate. During the Korean War, the Chinese got so tired of fighting with Marines that their commanders gave the order to avoid contact with "the crazy yellowlegs." (Marine units could be identified by their distinctive, khaki-colored leggings that wrapped tightly around their calves and kept their trousers from getting caught up in brush. Skiers today call them gaiters.)

Pretty cool, huh? You're in a war and you get a pass from combat because the enemy no longer wants to fight you? Nope. The Marines' commanders got wind of the Chinese order, and gave the order for the Marines to remove their leggings—and we have never put them back on ... which is a shame, because they look really cool, and lots of us join the Marines because the uniforms look so cool. Okay, not really—but looking good is the one bennie that comes with choosing the Marines.

So, as a former Marine, I decided to attack when it came to furthering my writing career. My humorous history of the United States was what I wanted it to be, and I didn't need an agent to send it to my publisher. Sure,

I could have gone back and worked on it for six months, but at some point, a writer has got to say, "That's my best." One's writing can *always* be improved, so where does the revision process end? Like planning for combat and arranging for the logistical resupply, editing could go on for years. Decades. Forever. Until they plant the unfinished manuscript alongside you in the grave. Eventually, however, *somebody* has got to say, "Fix bayonets and follow me."

Ergo, I decided to attack. The manuscript was launched north to my agent with a note suggesting that perhaps he could give it another go. Again.

Mr. Alexander, the VIP Booth Is This Way ...

While playing the waiting game, something exciting actually happened. It came as a one-two punch, and some subtle feelings of "real celebrity" percolated in my brain.

On a whim, I sent an article about my book to *Auburn Magazine*, the official alumni publication of my beloved alma mater. Since Auburn pumps out about twenty thousand grads a year, that adds up to about a million living graduates. If only ten percent of them are members of the alumni association, that's still a hundred thousand magazines shipping to the four corners of the nation. From here, let's throw in a reality check, and figure that only ten percent of those alumni would actually flip through the magazine, but that's still ten thousand fellow War Eagle eyeballs scanning the article about my book.

Next, I had to figure only ten percent of *those* folks would actually start reading a piece that didn't have the word *football* in the headline. That dropped us down to about a thousand. Of those folks, I estimated maybe ten percent of them would finish the copy-heavy article and look to see who wrote it, which dropped us to one hundred. Of those souls, probably ninety percent would want to kick my ass for taking up space that could have gone to discussing football, but the other ten percent might enjoy it, and think I'm a very fine fellow indeed. Of these ten folks, I guessed ten percent would buy the book and read it cover to cover ... and it was a longshot, but that person might know my stupid college girlfriend who dumped me, and might tell her that her prediction that I'd amount to nothing was wrong, and that I'd amounted to, well, more than nothing. That was exciting.

The next exciting thing came in the form of a phone call a few days later. It was none other than the director of the Auburn Alumni Association. What she said was ... words fail me.

She invited me to sit in the VIP booth at the Auburn versus LSU game.

Yes, that's right. Your pal, Mr. Drawer-Full-of-Rejection-Letters, and his beloved, long-suffering bride were invited to attend the Auburn/LSU game free of charge, seated in the VIP alumni box. Say it with me: Ka-ching!

Now, seeing as a critic of my first manuscript once dubbed me a "stereotypical, macho Southern male," I am aware that the thrill of this particular honor might not resonate with everyone, but let me assure you of this: Every fellow "stereotypical, macho Southern male" reading this book has now stopped reading and is at his computer furiously composing that novel he's been meaning to write. Think of it as, uh, the excitement Jill Biden might feel if Joe could make it through a press conference while sticking to the script.

Surely, this would be the beginning of great, great things.

The Hits Just Keep Comin'!

So, feeling like quite the VIP in the eyes of Auburn, I wasn't too surprised when a phone call came in from a very nice fellow named Brian who explained he was Auburn's director of something. He was going to be in Charleston and wanted to take me out to dinner! Well, hell yeah, of course he did—I was becoming a seriously important author.

I was already having a conversation with him in my mind's eye—the discussion I just *knew* was going to happen:

BRIAN: So, Prioleau, we want you to come this spring to speak to our graduating class, and allow us to bestow upon you an honorary doctorate. It'd be a real honor for us.

ME: My wife would need one, too.

BRIAN: Of course—we'd be pleased to include her.

ME: What else do you have for me, ol' fella?

BRIAN: Yes—well, of course, we'll be extending you an offer to serve as writer-in-residence emeritus, deus ex machina, forty-four magnum.

ME: And the honorarium would entail ...

BRIAN: Sadly, there'd be no salary, but there are football season tick—

ME: I'm in.

BRIAN: Great! Your seats will be next to Bo Jackson and Charles Barkley. Do you remember them? You were classmates.

ME: Well, my years in college were pretty focused on academics, and preparing to enter the Marine Corps, but no worries. I'm sure they're amiable blokes, whoever they are. Can I get some Auburn T-shirts, too?

So he and I got together for dinner and a beer. He was very pleased with the inn I'd recommended, and we got along famously. Then ... he told me his job entailed raising money for Auburn, and asked if yours truly might share some of my newfound riches. Sadly, Brian quickly found out what you already know: The financial difference between a rookie author and an aspiring author is that one has no money, and the other is aspiring to have no money. He took the news well, and felt so bad for asking that he gave me some of his pocket change.

Ka-ching!

THAT'S IT? YOU'RE BREAKING UP WITH ME?

The Pass ...

Despite all my frustrations with the "being published" process, my book sold well—very, very well for a rookie author. I felt sure the process would be easier the second time around, when my publishers saw my earning potential. I'd sent them my re-re-re-re-written humorous history of the United States, and felt confident about it; over the years, my skills as a writer had grown, and I felt the new edited version was even better than the first.

About a month after sending it in, an email arrived. I assumed it would be news of my vast advance, a national book tour, and maybe a picture of the CEO's lingerie-model daughter, who wanted to meet me.

Not exactly.

It said something along the lines of, "Not what we're looking for right now. We're going to give it a pass."

What it did *not* say included: "Thank you for making our company a lot of dough while you made some pocket change." It also failed to mention anything like "Not what we're looking for, but you're a damn fine writer and we think your style would work perfectly for a book about _____." It even lacked the words "Please stay in touch."

That was it: "We're going to give it a pass."

That put me back at square one. I'd officially gone from "published author" to "struggling writer" with the delivery of that one sentence.

All that Hollywood-version stuff? Poof. Vanished. Gone in seven words. That's a jagged pill to swallow.

But I did feel, in some ways, after thirty-some-odd years of dreaming and writing, I had reached the summit. I was published, and I had experienced the full-blown zippity freakin' doo dah of planting that flag. *Finally*, I got to tick that box.

But I also learned something along the way.

I liken it back to the mountain-climber concept: If you read Jon Krakauer's brilliant book *Into Thin Air*, you will discover a very curious thing. When climbers summit Everest—the undisputed heavyweight of vertical challenges—very rarely do they experience elation. There is no end-zone dance. There is no triumphant release. Meaning-of-life revelations are rare to the point of nonexistence. In reality, most climbers share only one feeling as they stand there: exhaustion. And exhausted, they turn and begin the perilous descent from the place that gave them no joy.

The joy they do feel comes later, when they're hanging around with other mountain climbers, because fellow climbers "get it." Together, they can bond over the accomplishment of reaching that joyless summit. They can share stories of climbs fair and foul, and revel in one another's tales. They can talk the lingo and laugh about things you and I would never understand. They are warriors of the ascent, and they share a bond of sweat and danger. And it is this bond—this understanding of shared suffering—that calls them back to the mountain, time and again. Like an infantry unit in combat, they do it "for the warrior to their left and their right." They are in a very tiny, very exclusive club ... a club even Bill Gates can't buy his way into.

But what about published authors? Where is *our* club? Where can I go to laugh and get drunk and lament the bewildering experiences of a rookie author's rookie year? Where can I find another rookie who will commiserate on the hours-invested versus net-income dilemma? I can't, of course. Yes, there are writers groups with wonderful people in attendance, but it's not *writing* I want to discuss—it's commiserating about the rookie year experience, and how hollow it turned out to be. It's hard to find those few souls, because there just aren't that many writers who've even had a rookie year. I want to bitch about the time on the summit, not the training techniques one needs to master to get there.

That is why, of course, I wrote this book. I want you, my fellow writer, to know what's behind the curtain, because it ain't much. And when you get published and find that out for yourself, odds are you won't find any kindred souls available for a bitch session. (I suppose you can always track me down and bitch. I'm on Facebook—in the event you haven't heard of it, that's the old people's social media.)

Listen: If you are a writer, write because you love it. Write for you. Write because it exorcises demons and lets slip angels from your soul. Write in hopes that your work will make it through the landmines and barbed wire that lie between you and the bookstore. But don't write book-length projects for money. There is none.

The big-publishing-house industry is built on this business model: Throw crap against the wall. Maybe one in five thousand books will stick, but when it does, the money-printing presses crank up. Remember: J. K. Rowling wrote *Harry Potter*, achieved unimaginable riches, and she got maybe fifteen percent of the profits. How much does that leave the publisher? I know you're a writer, but do the math. It's the math that keeps them throwing crap against the wall.

How, you might ask, can this business model be sustainable? Why haven't writers figured it out? Two reasons: For one, the publishing industry tends to play its cards very close to the vest, so there's a cone of silence engulfing the topic. And here's the big one: Many writers don't care about getting paid. Their reward is simply seeing their book up on the shelf—and that's understandable. That's fair. That's quite an exciting accomplishment.

But I'm in a different place from most writers. I've been a for-profit writer for my entire adult life, so my writing is associated with a paycheck. Yes, it's true that I wrote mostly for advertising clients, but that's how and where I came to understand the tricks of the trade: how to write in different styles, how to communicate in a limited amount of space, and how to avoid burying the lede. My experience made writing a book easier, and gave me a head start on developing the style and "voice" I now prefer to utilize.

So ... what's my advice to you?

First, you should continue to query agents. People *do* get struck by lightning every now and then, and you might just get struck, too. You'll have to have an agent to get your manuscript in front of a big publishing house, and while it's true some kinda-big publishers claim they'll take a look at an author-submitted project, they're mostly lying. You'd be better off using your time to write letters to your congressional representative—at least they'd get opened by someone before being ignored and thrown away. If you are determined—as I was—to be published by one of the "big boys," an agent is a hundred-percent must.

Your *best* odds of having your book published are by doggedly researching small publishing houses. If you put in the work, you'll find a publisher that loves your genre, even if it's Southern-gothic-romance-horror-crime fiction. As I said earlier, these are the people who publish for the love of the writing art, and actually do want to give voice to interesting, talented, undiscovered writers.

Want proof? You're reading it. No big publisher in history has ever published a nonfiction book critical of the publishing industry. No one. Ever.

Tara Tomczyk, owner/editor-in-chief of Blydyn Square Books, thought it was a cool idea, liked my writing style, and said, "Let's do it."

This does not mean smaller publishing houses aren't every bit as discerning about what they publish—perhaps they are more so, as they have neither the time nor the money to "throw stuff against the wall and see if it sticks." However, if you find a publisher who operates within your niche, you'll get a fair shake. If they bite, they personally work with you. It's certainly a fun and unique process.

And, of course, there's self-publishing. If you want more than a digital version, you'll need to pay someone to turn your manuscript into a book, but the good news is that writers no longer need to pay up front to print a lifetime supply. Most self-published books exist mainly (or only) in digital format, but you *can* sell paperback or hardcover copies, printing on demand. The book loiters somewhere in the proverbial cloud, and when someone makes a purchase on Amazon, the system is triggered, and the book is printed/bound/shipped by … a robot? Hell, I don't know. The point is: Self-publishing is a gamble, but at least you're gambling on yourself.

With my "for what it's worth" advice delivered, I will add that it took my rookie year to understand and embrace the fact that our craft isn't about the money, or fame, or adoring fans. It's about the process: bringing our ideas to life and pressing on up the mountain until we can say, "For this moment in my writing career, that's my best. I'm going to ski back down, catch my breath, and climb the mountain again."

EPILOGUE

Odds are, this book doesn't contain the realities you hoped it would.

The tales filling its pages certainly don't reflect the experiences I expected, back when my agent called and said he'd sold my manuscript. I thought … well, my thoughts have been covered in detail.

So, what are you supposed to take away from it? What nuggets are you going to glean from all these words?

Obviously, you can rest assured that what goes on behind Oz's curtain ain't what you thought it would be. It's a rough business.

Next, on a writers forum where I lurk from time to time, a frequent comment comes up that says approximately, "How do I make my protagonist better?" I never answer, because no one wants to hear the truth, which is: "Stop writing, read a hundred books in your genre, and highlight the things you like." Yes, I understand: As a writer, you want your God-given talents to flow from you, and you alone. Highlighting stuff and taking notes sounds like "cheating," but it ain't. Think of yourself as a college athlete—you've got to be coached and you've got to practice what you learn every day in order to make the pros.

In addition, being in a writing club is sometimes very helpful, if you go in with a thick skin. Insisting that the other members be tough on you is the only way you'll learn and improve.

On that same writing forum, the question often arises: "I want to write a book, but hate my writing. How do I get better?" Believe me, the answer ain't voodoo like "swing a dead cat around your head at midnight in a graveyard." It's writing a couple of million words and criticizing your own stuff. Ask yourself, "Why was that sentence good, but that one isn't?" I'll bet I've written fifteen million words in my life, and I still learn when I stop to self-criticize what's on my screen. This part of the art of writing usually isn't fun, but it can be: There's always satisfaction in transforming a mediocre sentence into a great one.

Another nugget I hope you've picked up is the need to ask yourself: "Do I really want to be a writer?" No one can offer real advice on that, but sitting down at the keyboard has got to be exciting for you. You need to lust after the hours you can commit to it. It's got to be fun, even without thinking about whether what you write might eventually get published. How many hours do you think Alicia Keyes sounded like crap on the piano? And how many hours did it take to go from crap to being Alicia Keys?

Thousands.

And, as mentioned earlier, the art she pursued enabled her to make an audience happy even before she achieved greatness … just walk into a party, sit down, and start playing. Immediately she's the center of attention and people are clapping after every song.

You and I will never get that.

Is that the validation you crave? Audible and immediate response to the art you worked so hard on? If it is, well, there's lots of fun stuff to pursue and do in life that doesn't involve being a stalker of your own keyboard. I'm not saying that in jest—if you're creative enough to write, you'd likely make a great photographer. Perhaps a painter. Or piano player. If you commit five hundred hours to learning a musical instrument, odds are you'll be good enough to play in public—and enjoy some of that validation. Five hundred hours as a writer? You're just getting started, and there's no guarantee you'll ever receive validating praise … not even from your mom.

If you'd like an easy way to see your byline in print, know that weekly newspapers are dying for content. Stop by and ask to see the editor—and volunteer to write a few stories for free. Ask if they have a topic or event they'd like covered, or pitch them on an idea. Note: You will need to spend a little time researching the "journalism writing style," but it's not hard—and add some of your creativity into your writing. If you do it right, they'll run it unedited.

As an added benefit, if you develop a relationship with the paper, you can go to businessman X in the local community, and say, "Hey, I'm in the public and media relations business. I think I can get a story in the paper about the cool stuff your business is doing. If I pull it off, my fee would be five hundred dollars." I've done it many times myself. Easiest money a writer can make.

Oh, and if you have success with the weekly paper, rest assured that you'll get a lot of press when your book comes out.

It's an old adage that great sentences make great paragraphs, great paragraphs make great chapters, great chapters make great books. And that's where you are, looking to get your first book published: Every sentence matters. Edit and revise and sweat until you reach the point where you think, "I can't believe I wrote that paragraph. It's perfect." Every paragraph won't be perfect, of course—there are lots of paragraphs in this book that could be better—but every paragraph needs to be the very best you can do. Once you gain a readership, then you'll enjoy the luxury of using a couple of chapters to build the story.

But for right now, as you search for an agent or a small publishing house, *abide by their exact guidelines.* Make your submission so good, it's like a punch to the face. In fact, every sentence you submit needs to make them feel like they've been punched by Mike Tyson ... for ten straight rounds.

Sure, there are writers out there who may have more God-given talent than you, but the real question is: "Can they *outwork* you?"

Therein lies the rub.

ACKNOWLEDGMENTS

Audrey Mullen of Advocacy Ink and Debbie Shaw at Auburn University—both played a huge role in the success of *You Want Fries With That?*

Mark Russell, my college roomie who's been cheerleading my writing for over thirty-five years

Charles Waring of the *Charleston Mercury* and Will Folks of FitsNews.com, for providing me with venues where I can rant

The late Champ Yarbrough, my lifelong friend, who introduced me to the genius of P. J. O'Rourke

Tiger and Polly Buxton of Buxton Books, and indie bookstore owners everywhere

Tara Tomczyk, the editor and fearless publisher of this book

My fellow writers, who are out there in the arena, faces marred by dust and sweat and blood, striving in a worthy cause

ABOUT THE AUTHOR

 **Prioleau Alexander** is a native of Charleston, South Carolina, a former Marine officer, and a graduate of Porter Gaud School and Auburn University.

He is the author of the nonfiction humor book *You Want Fries With That?*, which Pat Conroy described as "magnificent." His second book, *Dispatches Along the Way*, explores his pilgrimage across Spain on the Camino de Santiago, which caused his feet to hurt very badly.

He is a regular contributor to several regional publications, covering politics and nonfiction humor. He lives in Charleston with his wife, Heidi.